PYTHAGO

A concise accoun
and teachings of Pythagoras and
of his influence on Western
thought.

Also in this series:

ALCHEMY: THE GREAT WORK
Cherry Gilchrist

THE DRUIDS: MAGICIANS OF THE WEST
Ward Rutherford

FAIRY TALES: ALLEGORIES OF THE INNER LIFE
J. C. Cooper

THE GOLDEN DAWN: TWILIGHT OF THE MAGICIANS
R. A. Gilbert

THE INQUISITION: HAMMER OF HERESY
Edward Burman

MYSTICISM: THE DIRECT EXPERIENCE OF GOD
Michael Cox

SYMBOLISM: THE UNIVERSAL LANGUAGE
J. C. Cooper

PYTHAGORAS

Lover of Wisdom

by

Ward Rutherford

THE AQUARIAN PRESS
Wellingborough, Northamptonshire

First published 1984

British Library Cataloguing in Publication Data

Rutherford, Ward
Pythagoras
1. Pythagoras
2. Philosophers—Greece—Biography
I. Title
182′.2 B243

ISBN 0-85030-379-6

The Aquarian Press is part of the Thorsons Publishing Group

Printed and bound in Great Britain

Contents

PART ONE:
THE PHILOSOPHER IN HIS TIMES

1. Philosophy's Mystery Man

Pythagoras is the mystery man of Greek philosophy, a figure so shadowy, so shrouded in enigma and doubt that some have questioned his very existence and suggested he is a figure of pure legend. While so extreme a view can safely be rejected, one is compelled to recognize a total lack of certainty about the man, his life and his teachings. He had no amanuensis; no eye-witnesses have told us their stories. He left no writings of his own. We have not even the exiguous information of a gravestone to tell us his dates of birth and death. Was he sage or charlatan? A miracle-worker or a trickster? Was he a moral teacher or merely the focus of what we should today call a 'fringe cult'? All these views have been canvassed almost from his own day and are still with us.

His name, which means 'Mouth of Apollo', links him with the god and his sanctuary at Delphi. Originally the oracular shrine of the earth goddess Gaia, Apollo appropriated the sanctuary after slaying its guardian serpent – hence, the honorific title Python was given to him while his prophetic mediums were called the Pythia. In the lifetime of Pythagoras the Delphic Oracle was at the peak of an influence it exerted not only over the Greek city-states, but far beyond. The Lydian king Croesus and the Egyptian pharaoh Ahmose II sent tributes and consulted it.

The legend of the seizure of the shrine (it was probably re-dedicated to Apollo about 1500 BC) symbolizes a shift in

Greek religion from the feminine to the masculine dominated. However, the worship of Apollo soon became something more fundamental than a mere shift of gender. It was the beginning of a reformation that was to continue sporadically for centuries, reaching a fresh crisis about or before the time of Pythagoras. He was in the vanguard of these changes and so, on these grounds alone, it is not surprising to find his name associated with Apollo. If certain of his exegists are to be believed, he seems to have enjoyed a semi-official status in respect to the Delphic shrine, for he is credited with the authorship of at least one of the moral aphorisms written on its walls.

This Apolline link is carried even further by some writers, for whom he is the god's 'son', while others went as far as to declare that in Pythagoras was Apollo's actual living incarnation. He is also often spoken of as a *daimon* – that is to say, a being midway between the human and the divine.

However, while, on the one hand, we have those who carry adulation to the point of deification we also have, on the other, his contemptuous detractors. Heraclitus of Ephesus, probably a contemporary, cites him in proof of his contention that 'much learning does not each insight', for, out of his extensive study Pythagoras only 'contrived . . . a polymathy, a worthless artifice'. He was not alone in his denunciation. Zeno the Eleatic attacked the Pythagoreans in his book *Against the Philosophers.* Diogenes Laertius (*c.* AD 200–250) quoted a passage from Xenophanes of Colphon ridiculing the doctrine of transmigration of the soul. On seeing a man beating a dog, Pythagoras is alleged to have protested, 'Stop, do not beat him; it is the soul of a friend. I recognize his voice.' Comedians in the late fifth and early fourth centuries BC made jokes about a supposed ban on eating meat, such as the following side-splitter:

First Comedian: The Pythagoreans eat no living things.

Second Comedian: But Epicharides the Pythagorean eats dog.

First Comedian: Only after he's killed it.

As to Pythagoras's followers, they were often represented as a tribe of dirty, barefoot cranks, a species of antique hippy.

With the dense undergrowth of conflicting opinion already obstacle enough to any traveller seeking to discover the path to the truth, we have also to remember the various warnings issued by those who have trodden it before. W. K. C. Guthrie reminds us that since Pythagoreanism was as much a religion, albeit a mystery religion, as a philosophical school, its founder was bound to be seen as a prophet and venerated as such. This, carried to excess, led to discoveries being attributed to him for which he could not conceivably have been responsible. The readiest example is his famous 'Theorem', according to which the square on the hypotenuse of a right-angled triangle is said to be equal to the sum of those on the other two sides. This was known and employed by the Mesopotamians at least a millennium before the lifetime of Pythagoras, as we know from the translations of the cuneiform. It was, besides, a characteristic of the ancient world that it was generally believed that ideas, like wine, improved with age.

An illustration of this is Orpheus, prophet, singer and founder of the Orphic mystery religion. Known to us mainly as the inspirer of Gluck's *Orfeo* and, inappropriately enough, of the music for the French can-can, he was probably an historical figure whose lifetime pre-dated that of Homer (*c.*800 BC). Yet works bearing his name continued to appear well into the Christian era. According to a tradition going back to the fifth century BC, Pythagoras himself wrote under the name of Orpheus. It is little wonder, then, that the longer the period separating men from his lifetime, the more likely they were to call on his name in testimony, on even the most tenuous evidence of association.

By general consensus, however, Pythagoras committed nothing to writing under his own name. This is entirely consistent with a secrecy some found so impressive and others so exasperating. Porphyry mentions 'an exceptional silence', which makes it impossible to know what he taught, and the Pythagoreans were said to be 'more admired for their silence than the most famous orators for their speech'. Would-be disciples were made to swear a five-year oath of silence as part of their novitiate. Such practices, inimical to philosophy, were by definition part of the mystery religions, in which only those who had proved their reliability, discretion and dedication through a series of purificatory rituals were granted the final revelation.

How well the Pythagoreans' secrets were kept we have no means of knowing at this distance in time. We do know it made them a source for conjecture, gossip and slander, some of which has stuck, mud-like, down the centuries.

According to Diogenes Laertius no knowledge of Pythagorean doctrines was possible before the time of Philolaus, one of the original disciples. Unfortunately for us, his works, like those of two other disciples, Aristoxenus and Dicaearchus, are lost. So, too, are books by Aristotle and Democritus, while the work of a pupil of Plato's, Heraclides of Pontus, is known to us only from excerpts in other writers.

The most diligent search of the classical sources yields only a handful of brief references to Pythagoras and his followers. Plato's *Phaedo* is a description of the last day in the life of Socrates up to the moment he executed the death sentence of the Athenian court on himself by drinking the hemlock. Two characters, Simmias and Cebes are introduced and are said to be Thebans and pupils of Philolaus, making them second-generation Pythagoreans. Although there is no discussion of the philosophy, a careful reading of the work leaves an impression of Socrates's considerable debt to Pythagoras.

But by the lifetime of Plato (*c.*427–348 BC), Pythagoreanism had already undergone much modification and development. The passing of every year saw a growth in the accretion of legend round the founder's name while the iconoclasts became ever more indiscriminate in their attacks. Thus, for Plato's pupil Aristotle, the task of driving a mean course between these extremes was a considerable one and though he is our earliest source for events in Pythagoras's life, his scepticism about most of the legend comes through even in the few fragments we have.

The two biographies we possess in full, those of Porphyry and Iamblichus, did not appear until the third and fourth centuries of our own epoch: that is to say, some 800 years after the lifetime of Pythagoras. To rely on these as unreservedly as some writers have is rather like relying on a work by an Elizabethan for a biography of Alfred the Great.

In any case, both had axes of their own to grind. The

publication of their books coincided with the fourth-century pagan revival under Flavius Julianus, 'Julian the Apostate', whose personal hatred of the Christians was such he was prepared to give his full support to any assault upon their religion. The Neoplatonists, including Iamblichus and Porphyry, the latter already the author of a book entitled *Against the Christians,* led the attack. One of their strategies was to try to demonstrate that there was nothing unique in the mission, teaching or even the miracles of Jesus Christ; parallels could be found in antiquity, especially in the lives of austere and saintly pagans like Pythagoras.

* * * * *

The historian has not only the tangled undergrowth of differing opinion to chop away, he also has to try to reconcile flat contradictions between one account and another. A typical instance, though only one among many, is the Pythagoreans' vegetarianism. They believed in reincarnation and that the soul could return to earth in animal form – reason enough, it might be thought, for abstention from meat-eating, as it would be a form of cannibalism. Empedocles (*c.*490–430 BC), a philosopher, mystic and admirer of Pythagoras, took exactly this view; and the generality of Greeks must have regarded vegetarianism as a mark of the followers of Pythagoras or the jokes of satirists and comedians would have been pointless. Onesicritus, the Cynic philosopher and friend of Alexander the Great, is quoted by Strabo as declaring that Pythagoras ordered total abstention from animal food. Eudoxus, quoted by Porphyry, says the ban was carried so far that Pythagoras could not bear to have anything to do with those whose work brought them into contact with meat, such as cooks, butchers or hunters.

Yet elsewhere, Porphyry tells us the prohibition was not absolute. Athletes were urged to eat meat daily (though it is possible that this is a case of mistaken identity, as there was a second Pythagoras who was, in fact, a trainer of athletes). According to Aristotle the ban was partial, and included within its scope only the white cock, because it was sacred to the lunar deity, animals that had died, mullet, blacktail and egg-bearing creatures. Aristoxenus, whose circle of friends included some of the original disciples of Pythagoras, reports that he relished a meal of young pig and sucking kid. Iamblichus explains that it was permissible to eat those animals that were dedicated to sacrifice since the souls of men did not enter them, though of these it was improper to eat the loins, genitals, marrow, feet and head. To vex the question further, we have it on other authority that Pythagoras actually forbade animal sacrifice anyway!

Confusion confounded to the point at which the sceptic might well ask whether the investigation of Pythagoras's life and philosophy can be worth the candle?

I believe it can be for several reasons.

We have already seen that Pythagoras helped to determine the course of Greek philosophy – a fact that acquits him of Heraclitus's charge of charlatanism and of being a mere dabbler in such unprofitable areas as number-mysticism. If, as A. N. Whitehead says, the European philosophical tradition 'consists of a series of footnotes to Plato' and Aristotle was right in the contention that Plato was strongly influenced by Pythagoras, then surely this alone justifies our inquiry?

It may be that of the ideas attributed to him only a tiny proportion were rightly his. None the less, it is plain that he was believed to be their originator by men of considerable scholarship and discernment. To Empedocles, whose credentials still remain unchallenged and who probably came into contact with Pythagoreanism, at least indirectly, at an early stage in its life, its founder was 'a man of surpassing knowledge, who possessed vast wealth of understanding, capable of all kinds of cunning arts', who 'when he exerted himself with all his understanding easily did every one of all the things that are in ten of twenty human lives'.

And his influence has also been an enduring one. 'I was never so berhymed since Pythagoras' times,' says Rosalind in Shakespeare's *As You Like It,* 'that I was an Irish rat, which I can hardly remember.' This is an obvious allusion to the doctrine of transmigration. Only a few pages earlier, Duke Senior testifies to the hold that the notion of the Celestial Harmony had taken on the Elizabethan imagination when he comments, 'We shall shortly have discord in the spheres'. The same motif occurs in the famous night-scene in *A Merchant of Venice*, where Lorenzo tells his Jessica:

> Look how the floor of heaven
> Is thick inlaid with patines of bright gold!
> There's not the smallest orb which thou behold'st,
> But in his motion like an angel sings . . .

The reference is doubly interesting for Jessica was a Jewess and as she (and perhaps Shakespeare) knew, there had been considerable cross-fertilization between Greek and Judaic ideas when they met on the common ground of Alexandria in the first century AD.

From these and a host of other literary hints a measure of the *réclame* of Pythagoreanism in post-Renaissance England can be gathered. To men like John Dee and Robert Fludd, philosopher-scientists of international repute, Pythagoras was, like themselves, a magus.

Interest in him was by no means confined to England. Across Europe a band of esotericists, giants in whom philosophy, science and occultism were joined in a way not seen for centuries, were devouring every word they could find about him, at times with scant regard for authenticity.

He was numbered among the *prisci theologi*, an élite that included, besides Pythagoras, Hermes Trismegistus, Zoroaster, Orpheus and Plato, as well as Philolaus, the Pythagorean already mentioned. Pagans they might be; nevertheless, by their unblinkered observation of the natural world and the open-minded, incisive brilliance of their speculations, they were led to conclusions that prefigured the revelations of the Christian gospel.

But there was still another reason for making an effort to try and recapture at least a partial idea of Pythagoras and his teachings. Ignoring the praise of later generations – who might, after all, have been mistaken – and with every other possible allowance made, we are bound to recognize that if only a moiety of what was credited to him was true, he was so consummate and versatile a genius that one is immediately struck by the resemblance to the 'universal men' of the Renaissance, men like Leonardo, Michelangelo or Dante.

2. Greece in Pythagoras's Day

The resemblance between Pythagoras and the great men of the Renaissance is by no means coincidental. The Renaissance – literarily, the rebirth – was that moment at which the men of Europe, having rediscovered the banished learning of the past, were seeking to remodel themselves and their world according to the classical images Pythagoras himself had helped to shape.

But there was another, perhaps more fundamental reason for the similarity. Pythagoras was born towards the end of what historians have designated the Archaic Period, when Greece was beginning to move into the full richness of Classicism, a transition his lifetime bestrides. Many parallels can be drawn between Greece at this time of change and Italy in the period preceding the Renaissance. In both places and epochs it was a time of expansion. In Italy, this took the form of the larger towns spreading into the countryside to absorb the lesser ones, like creeping volcanic lava. In Greece the difficulty of feeding a growing population from limited resources of fertile land had been the spur to great migrations eastward, to the littorals of the Sea of Marmara and the Black Sea, and westward, to Sicily and the foot of Italy, while isolated trading-posts were established along the southern coast of what was then Celtic Gaul and as far west as Tarragona and Sagunto in Spain.

It also took the migrants to the Aegean Sea, whose islands down as far as Crete were gradually annexed, and then on to the mainland of Asia Minor along the fringes of what is now western

Turkey, but which was then known as Ionia.

The migrants came as warrior bands, led by men who believed themselves darlings of the gods, ordained to conquer and to rule. They became the kings of what were in Greece, as in *quattrocento* Italy, city-states, any tendency towards royal autocracy being curbed by a council of which all their brother commanders were members. The fruits of conquest included the parcelling-out of the land they had seized, a process which, by splitting territory into a number of smaller fiefs, encouraged the growth of clans and inter-clan conflict. When these became serious the king would be called upon to arbitrate. Inevitably, the loser was left with a fresh grievance and often both parties would disagree with the king's judgement, sometimes so strongly that this new resentment could supersede original quarrels and unite the aggrieved parties against the king. Such revolts of the nobility gradually eroded the authority of the kings to the point where they found themselves being removed from office, supposedly for abuse of power.

The aristocracy, who now took up the reins of government, were soon back at one another's throats. There was an additional, complicating factor. Even after the migrations, there was insufficient land to support the entire population adequately and large sections of it lived at best in conditions of hardship, at worst near to starvation, and were, in consequence, in a state of constant simmering, if not actual, rebellion. To provide enough food, external trade was necessary and this bred a merchant class. Since the trade was largely in finished goods, they, in due turn, depended on the skill of artisans and manufacturers. These emergent groups regarded themselves, with some justice, as contributing as significantly to economic life as the landowning aristocracy and demanded a say in government.

Their discontents were to some extent alleviated by admitting the wealthier merchants and artisans to the aristocracy, much as happened in Britain in the period following the Industrial Revolution. Henceforward, like their British counterparts, they regarded themselves as equals with the landed gentry; that is to say, they quickly began to believe that they, too, held their titles and positions by divine ordinance and were distinct from lesser mortals. It was from this class that the family of Pythagoras came, which may go some way towards explaining the élitism of the Pythagoreans.

All the same, the new men, once in government, breathed a much-needed vitality into it. Their day-to-day activities left them with comparatively large amounts of leisure, which they filled in many ways, including the practice of sport, so that the period saw the genesis of that cult of physical fitness and the worship of the human body we associate with Greece.

The grievances of the proletariat, however, were left unresolved, and it was certain that sooner or later those who saw them as a lever to political power would emerge. This actually began to occur in the late seventh and early sixth centuries BC. They were given the name of 'tyrants' and it is striking that when a similar group began to develop in pre-Renaissance Italy they were called the *signoria*, both names stemming from the word 'lord'. Despite the later connotations of the term, the tyrants were by no means invariably repressive (the yoke of government, whether that of king, aristocrat or tyrant was always lighter in Greece than among its eastern neighbours). Most often they held no official position and made no attempt to interfere in the state's laws or institutions. What they exercised was a kind of extra-legal authority, though in practice it was all-embracing just the same.

Once in power they had to keep the promises made to those who enabled them to seize it; but the debt once redeemed, and often only in the most token way, their style of government was largely indistinguishable from that of their predecessors, though it had the great merit of imposing a stability on the city-states under their sway. It did so in the teeth of the entrenched hostility of the landowners, who saw them simply as usurpers and panders to the mob.

The attitude of the merchant and manufacturing classes was probably more ambivalent. To those who had become most deeply imbued with the conviction of their hereditary right to rule, the tyrants were, naturally, as distasteful as they were to the aristocrats. For many, though, reality must have supervened. Stability brought prosperity and this was expended on capital projects. Greek architecture, another gift to humanity, burgeoned largely because of the tyrants' desire to give their success tangible expression. These activities inevitably enriched the merchants and artisans, and some of their new patrons even went so far as to create courts of artists, poets and philosophers around themselves.

But it also introduced a new element into the Greek view of the supernatural. Up till then, three seemingly irreconcilable attitudes had existed. The first, was the religion of the conquerors themselves, that of a Heroic Age. It explained life as men experienced it – a conflict with the hazards of hunger, the natural elements and war – much as one finds in the Anglo-Saxon epics. The omnipotent causers of these sufferings, insofar as they deigned to take notice of men at all, looked down on their struggles like a Roman matron at the amphitheatre. Life was a brief interregnum between two non-existences: that preceding birth and that of the grave, and to aspire to anything better was to set oneself up in perilous emulation of the gods, to commit the sin of *hubris*.

This attitude extolled only two virtues: personal courage and tactical cunning, like that of Agammemnon at Troy. In such an existence, the only consolations were those of feasting and a lust slaked indifferently on either sex. A man might try to prolong the period in which he could enjoy these pleasures by the meticulous execution of such obligations as sacrifice, but he knew from experience that there were no guarantees.

With the passage of time, this view degenerated into a purely state religion, with the king, the nobility or whoever was currently in power playing the central, invocatory role. In the great temples, the festivals were kept, the sacrifices slain and lip-service rendered to the presiding deity. If it was a unifying element, it was little more. It had nothing to say to the human condition.

Mystery Religions

The Greeks had never had the sort of self-abasing attitude to their religion to be found elsewhere. Their gods never inspired the paralysing awe of, say, those of Mesopotamia; and as early as the sixth century they were already questioning the adequacy of accepted belief. Xenophanes of Colophon attacked polytheism and its anthropomorphic tendency. He doubted the creation myths that had humankind springing, like plants, out of the earth. With extraordinary prescience, he suggested that they might have come from the sea and produced the fossils in evidence.

In fact, an alternative to orthodox religion already existed. The pre-Greek indigenous population of the region, the Pelasgians, had worshipped as gods the natural forces, in particular the Earth Mother. For them, religion did not express itself in sonorous but vapid liturgies in splendid temples. Their sanctuaries were in the remote, wild countryside where, by the light of flaring torches, they chanted and cavorted to the wail of flutes, the clash of cymbals and the remorseless, rhythmic beat of drums, working themselves up to a climax of such frenzy that women could dismember a live bull with naked hands to devour the gory flesh. This superhuman strength was taken as the proof of *entheoi*, possession by the god. It was typified in the cults of Gaia, the giver, through her daughter Ceres or Persephone, of the growing corn, and of Dionysus, the wine-giver, which had been developing as early as the times of Homer (*c.*ninth century BC).

It was orgiastic, even licentious, for as Euripides says in his *Ion*, 'Dionysus compels no woman to be chaste'. At the same time, it gave participants a real sense of communion totally missing from temple worship. By the time of Pythagoras, the cult of Gaia had evolved into the Eleusinian Mystery Religion.

The mystery religions, in contrast with normal Greek religion, were highly eclectic. Membership was reserved for those who had the right personal, temperamental and even ethnic qualifications: non-Greeks were not admitted to Eleusis, for instance. Such doctrinal base as they possessed was one which saw the worshipper less as a unit in a collectivity than as individual. He was to travel, step-by-step, through a succession of purificatory rituals that were always awe-inspiring and, in their latter stages, terrifying. *En route*, he was instructed in the teachings and mythology of the religion.

Final revelation, when it came, took the form of an actual encounter with the deity being invoked. The ordeals endured hitherto were as nothing beside this momentary glimpse of the numinous. Before it men trembled, sweated, convulsed, collapsed in dead faints. A number of contemporary parallels for such experiences can, of course, be found. Haitian and Dahomeyan voodoo or Brazilian *candomble* spring to mind, and we also have the eye-witness accounts of similar behaviour among those converted by the preaching of the Wesleys, the founders of Methodism.

In Eleusis, this single contact with the deity was considered enough to ensure salvation. It was a rebirth in which the initiate became the son of the divine mother and was adopted by the Immortals. In the graves of members of a secret sect discovered in Magna Grecia (now southern Italy) were sheets of thin gold giving the newly-released soul directions on how to negotiate the dangerous and difficult road to the Other World, avoiding all its pitfalls and detours. Once at his destination, and provided he had the right credentials for admittance, he would be welcomed with the words, 'Happy and blessed one, thou shalt be god instead of mortal.'

Orphism

Such manifestations as the mystery religions, however, were incapable of answering to another need of which men, with more time for reflection, were becoming conscious. Life, they saw, was grossly inequable. The wicked went unpunished; the good, unrewarded. Humanity must either resign itself to this state of affairs or look elsewhere for redress. Orphism, by introducing the concept of transmigration of the soul, was a move towards the latter. The wicked, it implied, might appear to thrive in this life, but would duly be punished in some future incarnation.

Orphism was still a mystery religion and thus open only to those who could afford to pay for initiation and the periodic renewal of rites. Orpheus himself was described by one critic as a singer and hawker of rites of initiation. Such men were as common in the Greece of the time as itinerant monks peddling papal Indulgences in the Middle Ages, and that they could survive by such means is testimony to the popular hunger for a more satisfying religion. Further, Orphism never possessed a morality in the strict sense. It dealt in a formal purity that viewed murder for gain and the breach of some minor taboo as equally sinful.

The seeds of something closer to a true personal morality came as the cult of Apollo developed, though it was to be a long time before it evolved into anything we should recognize by the name. From his myth came the previously unheard of notion that even a god must – and could – atone for the shedding of blood. After killing the Python, Apollo went into exile in Thessaly, living the life of a shepherd (thereby earning himself the title of Nomios, the Guardian of Flocks). The importance of this act can hardly be overstated for, if expiation were possible, humanity was no longer, as in the past, the plaything of the gods. A tacit contract existed. What was more, expiation was quite different in quality from the offering of sacrifice, which was no more than the giving of a gift in the hope of its return as divine favour.

Hyperborean Apollo

The French scholar Georges Dumezil claims to have isolated three main groupings of gods among the Indo-European peoples of which the Greeks, like ourselves, were one. They correspond to the three main elements in Indo-European society – the knightly, the magical and the agricultural, and are the gods of war, of shamanism and of fertility. Apollo, as Mircea Eliade points out in his *Shamanism*, is the most markedly shamanistic of all the Olympians, since he, like the shaman, forms the bridge across the gulf that separates the Two Worlds. The goddesses of fertility (like Demeter or Persephone) may be invoked to bless the sowing and the harvest, or the gods of war (like Ares) to favour the arms of votaries; but it is only through the gods like Apollo that the divine will is made known to men.

It is not, therefore, surprising that the walls of the temple at Delphi should have been adorned with a series of aphorisms: 'Know Thyself', 'Nothing in Excess', 'Curb the Spirit', 'Observe the Limit', 'Hate Hubris', 'Keep a Reverent Tongue', 'Fear Authority', 'Bow before the Divine', 'Glory not in Strength', 'Keep Women under Rule'. Traditionally, these were the work of an apocryphal Seven Sages, an elect that numbered Thales, said to have been one of Pythagoras's instructors, among its members. According to some sources Pythagoras himself had a hand in them, and certainly the injunction to 'keep the limit' has a profoundly Pythagorean ring. Whoever was responsible, and as much as our age might take issue with the sympathies of some of them, they are none the less moral statements in that they are exhortations to certain kinds of conduct in life; they therefore differ from the shibboleths of ritual applicable only to certain given sets of circumstances.

It is wholly consistent with his character of the god-who-speaks-to-men that as Phoibus, Apollo is linked with the sun and light, that light being as much mental and spiritual as physical. However, it is not as the Enlightener, the Serpent-Slayer or the Guardian of Flocks that Pythagoras was devoted to him. It was, in particular, as the Hyperborean Apollo.

The Hyperboreans were the inhabitants of a legendary country beyond the North Wind where spring was perpetual, skies cloudless and the earth yielded two harvests a year. There men not only lived for a thousand years, they also possessed an extraordinary wisdom that had been vouchsafed them by the gods themselves. It was, in some versions of his myth, the land from which Apollo hailed.

The Hyperboreans were said to stand in a special relationship to the Greeks. Herodotus describes how each year they sent gifts wrapped in straw to Apollo's mythical birthplace, Delos, and it was generally agreed that during his annual absence from Delphi, it was to his northerly home that Apollo returned.

3. Early Life

Pythagoras was probably born about the year 570 BC and the place was certainly Samos, part of Ionia. The island, which is only half a mile off the Asiatic coast, was one of the places settled in the seventh century. The inevitable myth surrounds its foundation. No less inevitably Pythagoras's more idealizing biographers associate his family with this event. In one such story, an ancestor, Ancaeus, 'son of Zeus', who dwelt at Same in Northern Greece, was instructed by the Delphic Oracle to colonize the isle of Phyllis and rename it after his own city. He did so, making the mandatory call at Delos, Apollo's birthplace, on the voyage to his new home.

What we know for sure is that, just as the first settlers in the New World tried to build an image of the civilization they had left behind on an alien shore, so too did the Ionic Greeks, who, like all colonizers, quickly came to regard the bringing of their culture to remote places as a divine mission. They had some reason for pride in their achievement. Even by this early date the succession of poets they had sired included Hesiod and Homer, and while Pythagoras is often regarded as the founding father of philosophy, and sometimes as the inventor of the word, he had been preceded in that same Ionic world by Thales, Anaximander and Anaximenes.

As to his fellow-islanders themselves, they had acquired a high reputation as architects and engineers. Their island was one of the legendary birthplaces of Hera (another was Argos), as well as the place where her marriage to Zeus had been consummated. According to Herodotus, the temple of Hera at Samos was comparable with the temple of Artemis at Ephesus and one of the Seven Wonders of the Ancient World. Their engineers had been responsible for extensive projects, which Lawrence Durrell describes as among the greatest feats of the time, including a harbour mole and a tunnel to carry drinking water. Traces of both can still be seen, though of the Heraion all that remains is its site on a headland. Their fame had obviously spread beyond their island, for they built a second Temple of Hera in the Egyptian city of Naucratis, where there was a Greek concessionary trading-post, as well as a bridge across the Bosphorus.

* * * * *

In Pythagoras's time, as now, philosophy was concerned with ultimate reality, though the divisions between it and what we should call 'natural science', the study of phenomena subdivided into various disciplines, had not then taken place. The philosopher looked on the microcosmic as much as the macrocosmic as his domain and often freely extrapolated from one to the other.

This tendency, much in evidence in Pythagoras, is one of the several characteristics that need to be taken into account in any attempt to understand his time.

But it is equally important to recognize the depth and breadth of the gulf that separates ancient Greek from our own Northern European modes of thought. Acquaintance with Greek classicism and the assimilation of so much of it into the fabric of our civilization has led to an illusory feeling of familiarity. Socrates, Plato, Aristotle; Euripides, Sophocles and Aeschylus can seem less remote than Langland, Chaucer or Bocaccio. The former have been nordicized to the point at which the Germans could (and, in some cases, still can) deceive themselves that the Classical Greeks were their own ancestors! They were not. They were and still are a Mediterranean people and the Victorian expression 'the Near East', which encompassed such places as Greece and Turkey-in-Europe, far more accurately evokes the true image. Compared with the grey and misty north, theirs was a brilliant, even gaudy world. Athens, and the smaller towns and cities, were places of palm trees, buildings with low-pitched roofs where a stray camel would not have seemed out of place. And in the time of Pythagoras, the Greeks looked eastward for their inspiration, copying freely the arts and the ideas of places like Egypt, Persia and Babylon.

One reason for this was, of course, that geographically and climatically they were much the same. This allowed for a life-style totally different from that of our own chilly region. The Greek, though not unacquainted with winter cold, dwelt for much of the year in a dazzling, all-revealing sunlight. Where the Northern European, because of the caprices of weather, had to provide shelter for many of his activities, the Greek could pursue them in the open. Schools, compulsory for boys, were gatherings round their teachers on any suitable plot of ground. The dramas of the great writers were performed under the sky in vast auditoria like that at Epidaurus. It was possible, not only to eat, but to cook meals *al fresco*. A wineshop or taverna was (as many of them are still) no more than a few tables set in the shade of a tree.

The ancient capital of Samos, since renamed Pythagorion in honour of its most illustrious son, looks straight across to the Asiatic coast. Like most Greek cities, it would have consisted of two elements: a religious centre, based on the temple, and a governmental and commercial one, based on the *agora* or marketplace. This comprised an arcade or *stoa*, where regular tradesmen and probably certain artisans had their shops, and an open square where farmers and peasants from the surrounding countryside, as well as fishermen straight from their boats, would come to sell their wares. A second-millennium frieze from Thera in Crete shows such a scene – a naked fisherman holding strings of mackerel in each hand, while squid adorn his head. Fish, flavoured with herbs, coated with olive oil and grilled on wood or charcoal, still forms an important part of the Greek diet. Meat was a luxury. But, whatever the fare, it would have been accompanied by copious draughts of wine, Samian being renowned down to the times of Lord Byron.

Besides its other functions, the *agora* of a Greek city, like the

Roman forum, served as a meeting place at which ideas on every subject under the sun were thrashed out. The Stoics took their name from the fact that they gathered with their disciples in the *stoa*; Socrates and Plato both held forth in the *agora* at Athens and there is no reason to suppose it was any different in Ionia at the time of Pythagoras.

His father, Mnesarchus, is variously described as a gem-carver and as a *toreutes* – that is, a worker in ivory and precious metals. This might go some way towards explaining the veneration of Apollo, for as god of the sun he was also master of gold, which the sun was believed to engender, as the moon, the domain of his sister Artemis, engendered silver.

However, other writers tell us that Mnesarchus was a merchant, and it is, of course, conceivable that he followed more than a single profession, or pursued one and then the other. If he was trading in metal, then he would probably have travelled to the Greek trading-post at Massalia (now Marseilles) and possibly as far as Cornwall or the southern coast of Ireland. It is also likely that his son followed in his father's footsteps. This would have been in accordance with a tradition institutionalized by King Solon of Athens and there is evidence that he had some kind of artistic and craft training, as well as a considerable knowledge of business, shipping and sea-routes.

His mother is said to have been a woman called Parthenis, meaning virgin, but when his father was told by the Delphic Oracle that she was going to bring forth a son by Apollo, she was renamed Pythais in his honour. Such stories of divine progenitors are common enough. Aethra, mother of King Theseus of Athens, was said to have conceived by the sea-god, Poseidon, after visiting his temple on the island of Poros, though – which is also common – Theseus also had a mortal father in the shape of King Aegeus. What one has to conclude is that there was a belief in a kind of dual generation, one physical and the other spiritual, and it is not surprising that those who sought to turn Pythagoras into a semi-deified prodigy should attach such beginnings to him. But the veracity of the whole story is somewhat shaken by other writers who say he also had two brothers, Euonomus and Tyrrhenus.

His father was almost certainly not Greek. For some writers

he is a Syrian, for some a Phoenician from the city of Tyre; for others, an Etruscan. If the last is true it might account for the Orphic elements with which Pythagoreanism is shot through, for Etruria was a major centre of Orphism.

Guthrie (in *Orpheus and Greek Religion*) sees Orpheus as a religious reformer and prophet who set out to purge the cult of Dionysus of its orgiastic excesses. He was killed by being torn to pieces by the Maenads, the ecstatic women-followers of Dionysus, allegedly for urging the worship of Apollo. He may have written works of his own, though much that bears his name was the product of others, including, as we have seen, possibly Pythagoras himself.

It was not until the sixth century, however, that Orphism began to emerge as a significant movement. Its doctrinal basis are the so-called Orphic Rhapsodies, no longer existing in complete form. These include an elaborate account of the creation of the gods, the world and humanity that is substantially at odds with that given by Hesiod. In this there was at the beginning an effable One, combining with himself/herself liquid and solid. From this mud-like form came a serpent, one of whose three heads was that of a bull and another that of the god Chronos (Time). His offspring was Aither (the air or 'Divine Breath'), out of which Chronos formed the World-Egg and whence came the first of the gods, whose numerous names include Dionysus, Eros and Phanes or the Light – the name by which he is usually known to the Orphics. Being hermaphroditic, he bore a daughter, Gaia (the Earth), and a son, Ouranos (the Heavens), from whose loins sprang the unruly Titans.

Another daughter, Night, took over from Phanes the task of creation and a succession of supreme gods came after her; but at each new generation the world vanished and had to be refashioned, a task for which Zeus, its final remaker, needed the advice of Night. By his union with Demeter, Zeus became the father of the lovely Persephone, whom he ravished incestuously. From her womb came a reborn Dionysus.

However, Persephone's adultery had inflamed the jealousy of Hera, Zeus's true wife, who with the Titans as her accessories, encompassed the destruction of the child-god. By the use of pretty toys they won his confidence, killed and dismembered him. Observing the crime, Zeus dispatched Apollo to collect his remains and carry them to the sanctuary at Delphi. But murder had not been enough for the Titans, they compounded their crime by feasting on the body, so that all Apollo was able to save was his penis (or, in some versions, his heart). From it Zeus recreated him, but still indignant at the outrage of the Titans, he destroyed them with his thunderbolt. Out of the ashes there sprang a new race, part Titanic, but because of their ingestion of the slaughtered Dionysus, also part divine.

This was mankind.

The Orphic Rhapsodies are, of course, a mish-mash of elements drawn from so many sources that one cannot help wondering if one of their original purposes was not an attempt at synthesizing the various creation myths which, as a sea-going people, the Greeks had picked up on their travels. The idea of life emerging from the primeval slime is to be found in Egyptian cosmology, for instance. The World-Egg occurs in that of the Phoenicians and of the far earlier Old Europeans of the Balkan area, whence it could have reached Thrace, the land of Orpheus.

The theme of dismemberment and god-eating recalls the worshippers of Dionysus, whose victim was a live bull and whose savage practices, if Guthrie is right, Orpheus was trying to stamp out. Its first home is thought to have been Crete, the centre of bull-worship, and it is noteworthy that one of the three heads of the world-serpent is that of a bull.

Of more direct import, however, are the moral overtones of the tale, with its nascent hints of a doctrine of original sin and an inner conflict between the Titanic and the divine in every human. Orphism developed a detailed rule of life that it enjoined on its followers. This included prohibitions on meat and bean eating, both later to become Pythagorean, as well as a belief in the transmigration of the soul. According to Orphic teaching, at death the individual soul went down to the realm of Hades – whose queen was Persephone, the daughter of Zeus. There it was tried and consigned to an Other World existence befitting past conduct before being allotted a new mortal span. The wheel rotated nine times (the figure is debated) before the final destiny of the soul was decided.

Though in the existing versions of the Rhapsodies, Apollo plays a very subsidiary role (in some he does not appear at all and Athena rescues the divine member), there are several intimations of his presence. The customary Orphic name for Dionysus, Phanes, the light, is similar to that accorded to Apollo. There is also every indication that Orpheus gave him special veneration and expected his followers to do likewise, while Guthrie points to hints that at some early point Apollo and Dionysus were one and the same.

* * * * *

Of the education of Pythagoras little is known. One writer names his teacher as the minor poet Kreophylus. However, since he was a contemporary of Homer, others, realizing the anachronism, have suggested that he was really the pupil of one of Kreophylus's descendants, the sage Hermadamas, who was a musician as well as a poet. Other accounts say that the family was too poor to afford formal education and that Pythagoras was apprenticed to his father, for whom he acted as bookkeeper – the origin of his interest in mathematics. Though he may have acted in such a capacity, perhaps because of a natural bent for arithmetic, it is difficult to reconcile family poverty with other information.

It is also said that Pythagoras had contact with Thales, Anaximander and Anaximenes, as well as with Pherecydes of Syros. That he was Pherecydes's disciple – and on the evidence, a devoted one – is possible and it is interesting that Pherecydes spent his declining years in Delos, Apollo's birthplace. The encounters with Anaximander and Anaximenes can, at best, have been only fleeting ones and are probably mere conjectures based on similarities to be found in all three. For instance, Anaximander, like Pythagoras, was involved in astronomy and cast horoscopes.

On his physical appearance the records are no more reliable. Those who sought to portray a figure of bewitching good looks belong to the mythologizing school, that which declared him the 'son' or 'incarnation' of Apollo, a god who was always portrayed as the embodiment of male beauty. The graphic delineations of a bearded and be-turbanned prophet are works of pure imagination, and even the coin portraits, which Guthrie takes as genuine, have had doubt cast upon them. For the tradition of 'the long-haired Samian' found in several sources some licence exists, as long hair was often the mark of the philosopher-magus.

There is, of course, the 'golden thigh' mentioned by Aristotle and said to be the mark of Apollo's special regard. In all likelihood it was just what Gorman (*Pythagoras*) suggests – a birthmark.

Pythagoras may well have married while still in Samos, as his compatriot, Duris, credits him with a son, Arimnestus. Late accounts give him a wife, Theano, daughter of Brontinus, after his move to Magna Grecia. There he is also supposed to have had a son, Telauges, and a daughter, Damo, both prominent in local affairs.

Stories of his setting himself up as a teacher early in life, using a cave as a lecture-theatre, are dubious as, at this stage, he does not seem to have regarded his own education as complete and would not, therefore, have made himself an educator of others.

The landowning aristocracy had managed to cling to power longer in Samos than in many other places. However, the youth of Pythagoras saw its decline, bringing with it the sort of political upheaval other places had endured.

The crisis could not have come at a worse time. Cyrus, King of Persia, having consolidated Media into his domains, had also subjugated Assyria, thus creating one single, vast province. This new and powerful neighbour was seen by Croesus, king of Lydia, as too great a potential threat to be ignored and, having visited Delphi where he was told 'he would destroy an empire', he believed he had providential licence to take up arms. The Oracle proved right; an empire was destroyed – his own. Lydia, then the Greek coastal cities, fell to Cyrus.

It was in these circumstances that Polycrates seized power in Samos about the year 538, when Pythagoras was in his early thirties. The tyrant at once looked to the island's defences, building galleys of 150 oars and an army of a thousand bowmen. He also instituted a network of alliances with those who shared his fear of Persia and succeeded not only in keeping Samos independent, but even in increasing its influence and wealth, much of the latter coming from the piracy for which the island was notorious.

Though he surrounded himself with artists and poets, among them Anacreon, Polycrates was luxurious and sensual; Pythagoras was an ascetic, so that his acceptance of the regime can never have been entirely wholehearted, and when he evinced a desire to travel Polycrates appears to have acted more or less as his sponsor, providing him with a letter of introduction to the Egyptian pharaoh Ahmose II, though this may have been a subterfuge to be rid of him and some commentators have suggested that Pythagoras's journeys were actually a form of banishment.

He is said to have taken three valuable cups with him to pay for incidental expenses while abroad. Since he came of a family which must at least have had contacts among craftsmen who made such articles, this sounds plausible.

His journeys may well have included a visit to Crete, where he was initiated into the cult of Idaean Zeus. The preparatory rites included nine days of solitary meditation in one of the caves on Mount Ida as well as the symbolical enactment of his own death and rebirth, an event whose significance will be clear later. In myth, the caves of Mount Ida were the place where the god's mother, Rhea, concealed the new born Zeus from his angry father, Kronos, whom he was ultimately to castrate with a sickle. Some have asserted that the island was the home of the purest form of Orphism and there are certainly so many parallels between this story and that of the Orphic Dionysus that they can be assumed to have had the same origin.

The island had been the site of bull worship from Minoan times (2400–1200 BC) and the bull is itself associated with both Dionysus and Zeus. Furthermore, the name by which the latter is most often called by the Orphics is the Cretan one, Zagreus. This associates him with Mount Zagros on the frontier of Assyria and Media, providing further evidence of Magian and Babylonic elements in the Orphic myth.

A visit there by Pythagoras is, therefore, highly probable, though whether it actually occurred at the beginning of his odyssey or at some later stage cannot be certain.

There was also another encounter, ascribed by some witnesses to a later date but which, since it must have had a profound effect on the formation of Pythagoras's ideas, seems more likely to have taken place earlier. This was his meeting with the mysterious Abaris, described as a Hyperborean priest and certainly associated with Apollo who, it is said, sent him to seek out Pythagoras. He recognized him as the incarnation of the god by the token of his golden thigh. Some witnesses go so far as to state that Abaris put himself under Pythagoras's tutelage.

The actual existence of the Hyperboreans has never been incontrovertibly proved or disproved, and the Greeks often confused the issue by using the name very loosely, even applying it to their own countrymen who worshipped Apollo in his Hyperborean guise. There were substantial communities of such worshippers among the colonies on both sides of the Sea of Marmara and on its islands. Abaris may, therefore, have been a priest from one of their temples, though Herodotus calls him a Scythian and this, too, is possible. The Scythians, inhabitants of a broad tract of land that extended to the Black Sea, also had another homeland in the depths of Siberia that had remained inhabited. Here they were believed to be in contact with the Hyperboreans.

By an even wider extension, the word was also used to cover any whose beliefs centred on a solar deity. Among this legion could be placed the Chaldeans with their Shamash, who shares many of Apollo's characteristics, or the Magian Ahuramazda. Both, however, are poor candidates as they were well enough known to the Greeks to have been specified.

A further intriguing possibility remains: the Celtic god Belenos (or Beli) also bears a striking resemblance to Apollo. Can it be, then, that Abaris is exactly what Hecateus (*c.* 500 BC) says he was – a Druid? It is not quite so far-fetched as might at first appear. The same writer, in another passage, identifies the Land of the Hyperboreans with an island opposite the north coast of Gaul that can only be Britain. It was, he declares, the birthplace of Apollo's mother, Leto. He goes on to describe a great temple on this mythical island in terms that leave no doubt that he is referring to Stonehenge. Every nineteen years, the length of a Druidic epoch, 'Apollo' manifested himself to its people amid great celebration.

The Druids, like Pythagoras, believed in transmigration, and Strabo (60 BC–AD 19) has him as their instructor in the doctrine. This is plainly nonsense, for not only is the Druidic belief much older, it is also quite different in character; and against Hecateus's thesis it must be pointed out that every indication is that to have merited the name of 'the People from Beyond the North Wind', the Hyperboreans would surely have had to have come from somewhere far more remote than Britain, while Leto is generally considered to have been an Asiatic goddess.

For all this, the story of a Druidic link is strangely persistent. Another source has Pythagoras studying the teachings of the Brahmins and Gauls: the second can only mean the Druids. That there was an encounter is by no means impossible for, as we have seen, the Greeks traded with the Celtic lands.

4. The Exile

In due course, Pythagoras arrived in Egypt, probably by way of the Greek emporium at Naucratis. His destination makes him appear to be taking the advice of Thales, but this is not necessarily so. It was the general Greek belief that their religion had originated in Egypt, and for this reason Pythagoras was not alone in making such a pilgrimage.

It must soon have become apparent to him that not even the good offices of the pharaoh were sufficient to gain him admission to the confidence of the Egyptian priests, the object of his journey. But after several fruitless attempts, he was finally accepted at the temple of Diospolis.

Precisely what he learned from the priests of Diospolis can only be surmised. With the belief that the Egyptians were the originators of their religion went a Greek conviction that their priesthoods consisted of men of surpassing wisdom. The Athenian orator Isocrates (436–338 BC), declared that the philosophy of Pythagoras was based on what he had learned from the Egyptians, while Herodotus asserts, wrongly, that the Egyptians shared the Pythagorean belief in reincarnation and, in consequence, abjured animal sacrifice. This, he says, is the reason why the Pythagoreans did the same.

What the Egyptians did teach was that on death the soul was arraigned for trial and rewarded or punished for deeds performed in life. This, of course, closely reflects the Orphic doctrine. They also believed in Ma'at, a concept of universal order as the frame into which everything, including individual human acts, fitted. The obvious counterpart to this is the Pythagorean Cosmos. Other Egyptian beliefs with Pythagorean homologues were a prohibition on burial in wool and on eating beans.

While the possibility that Pythagoras may have borrowed these ideas directly from the Egyptians cannot be entirely discounted, it is equally possible that the Egyptians themselves may have borrowed from a much older third source, one from which the same ideas may also have penetrated Orphism. The notion of Cosmos, for instance, is of very great antiquity and is to be found, in one form or another, in many cultures.

* * * * *

In 525 when Cambyses, son and successor of Cyrus, conquered Egypt, Pythagoras appears still to have been in the country and, we are told, was taken captive by the invaders. It is difficult to understand why, since he was the citizen of a neutral power, and in some versions it is stated that his ship fell victim to pirates while he was travelling. In any event, it seems to have been a blessing in disguise, for we next find him in Persia, where he came into contact with the Magi, the followers of Zoroaster. We even have those who make him the prophet's disciple, an extraordinary feat since, though we have no precise date for Zoroaster's death, it occurred not later than 1500 BC – that is to say, a thousand years earlier. The meeting was obviously interpolated in an effort to explain the various apparent similarities between Zoroastrianism and Pythagoreanism.

Some accounts say Pythagoras was taken to Babylon, by this time under Persian domination, where his teacher was one Zaratas the Chaldean, a possible source of the confusion with Zoroaster. In one sense, it is immaterial. The Magi were, in origin, Medians (one theory of their name is that it was derived from that of a Median tribe). The Chaldeans had always provided the intelligentsia of Babylon, including its priesthood. The Babylonic territories abutted Media and they must have influenced one another considerably. The Greeks, with their sloppiness about terminology, could well have used the word

'Chaldean' in relation to Zaratas meaning simply that he was someone who had adopted ideas that were generally thought to be Chaldean.

Pythagoras's own interest in astrology and numerology, even if it was not first aroused by these encounters, could well have been developed through them, as the Chaldeans and the Magi were experts in both. The latter, after all, were the wise men who recognized the significance of the Star of Bethlehem and went in search of the infant Christ. The Babylonians had gone so far as to assign numerical values to the gods, planets and elements. This, as we shall see, had a Pythagorean echo.

The Magi employed a ritual drug, *haoma*, extracted from one of the plants of the *Ephedraceae* family, whose purpose was to induce trance and vision. This may have suggested to Pythagoras the use of a concoction the Greeks called *kykeon* (= disorder) for the same purpose. The recipe is given by Porphyry as equal parts of opium poppy seeds, sesame and the bark of squill, and he says that Pythagoras was introduced to it in Crete.

Hints that Pythagoras's itinerary included a visit to India can safely be disregarded and were probably another attempt to account for certain elements in his philosophy, this time those that seemed to parallel those of the Hindus. According to Diogenes Laertius, who calls in witness lost works by Aristotle and Sotion of Alexander, the Indian 'Gymnosophists' (= naked wise men) were one of the four barbarian schools with whom philosophy originated, the others being the Magi, the Chaldeans and the Druids. This would make it appear logical that Pythagoras, having studied the others, would not omit the Indians. It was not, however, until the times of Alexander the Great (356–323 BC) that the routes to the Indian subcontinent were opened to Greek travellers.

* * * * *

His voyaging at an end, Pythagoras returned to Samos. The date we are given is 515 BC, and though by no means impossible, it would mean he was about fifty at the time.

It would also make his absence one of about twenty years duration. This was a period regarded as being particularly significant to the ancients (it has been suggested by some scholars that originally the period was nineteen years and that this was connected with the interval between eclipses, another highly significant period). However, this very fact arouses the suspicion that some of his biographers may deliberately have extended the length of time. It would also have helped to demonstrate the thoroughness of his studies.

Soon after his return we again have him teaching. This time his students gather about him at a natural arena, while the sage himself and some select students are said to live in a cave.

His sojourn in his native island was brief. It may have been another case of the prophet finding no honour in his own country, or else, as Iamblichus tells us, it was because the Samiots disliked his symbolistic style. But equally, it may have been that in a place where, under the licentious Polycrates, luxury ruled, the austerity of Pythagoras was an affront.

Or there may have been a purely practical reason: the increasing menace to Samos from Persia and the likelihood of a successful invasion. In Herodotus's *Histories*, the Samian tyrant was tricked into the hands of Cambyses, who crucified him and installed his own puppet in his stead. Pythagoras, though naturally credited with prophesying these disasters, may simply have been drawing the logical conclusions from the trend of events.

Among family friends was Democedes, Polycrates's personal physician and later, because of his reputation, to become physician to Darius, the future king of Persia. Democedes was a native of Croton (now Crotone) in Magna Grecia on the boot of Italy. Croton was renowned as a health resort and possessed a medical school that claimed to produce the best physicians in Greece. But it may have had a greater recommendation for Pythagoras: it was a centre of Orphism and the worship of Apollo, on the basis of whose oracular instruction the city had been founded, and, of course, as Alexikakos, the god himself was credited with curative powers.

Croton

The leaders of Croton must have been apprised of the arrival of Pythagoras in about the year 518, and to have welcomed it, for they seemed to have formed something like a reception committee. It may well have been that he had already acquired something of a name and that this preceded him; in any case, they may have seen him as the bearer of an Ionian enlightenment by which their own city had largely been bypassed. It is also said that he showed them his 'golden thigh' and was at once accepted as under the special protection of Apollo.

Although undoubtedly prosperous, Croton was at the time badly demoralized. About 530 BC, it had joined with two of its neighbours, Sybaris and Metapontum, in a war against a fourth, Siris. Despite the military assistance that Siris received from the city of Locri, the confederacy triumphed, whereupon Croton turned on the Locrians to punish them for aiding the Sirisians, only to be defeated at the Battle of the River Sagra. It was not only an unexpected, but a double humiliation. The Crotoniate forces were numerically far superior and they prided themselves on their athletes (at one Olympic Games its runners had taken all seven first places).

This recent defeat could well have been one of the reasons why the arrival of Pythagoras seemed so timely, for the Crotoniates, unable to believe their failure was due to themselves, ascribed it to the invocation of supernatural assistance by their foes. The Locrians, when they had realized they were about to be attacked by the far stronger Crotoniates, had applied to their old allies, the Spartans. They were otherwise engaged and instead sent as reinforcement the Dioscuri, the twin-hero sons of Zeus by Leda, identified with the constellation of Gemini. Clinging to them, besides an aura of divinity, was that of magic. One of their manifestations was as 'St Elmo's Fire', the luminous electrical discharge sometimes to be seen playing round the rigging of ships and taken by sailors as the presage of good weather. Their magical character was amply demonstrated in their appearance and conduct on the banks of the Sagra where, with scarlet cloaks streaming behind them, they appeared on their milk-white steeds first in this then in that part of the battlefield, ensuring victory. Their presence was said to have been conclusively proved to Crotoniate satisfaction by one of their wounded who was spirited from the fray to the oracular shrine of the Dioscuri in Sparta and there healed before being returned home, equally miraculously.

If, as at least some of the evidence suggests, Pythagoras had already acquired a reputation for occult powers, he would obviously have been particularly welcome to the Crotoniates at this low point in their fortunes, if only as a counter to the magic of others.

He seems to have immediately set about a rekindling of national spirit. Soon after his arrival he was invited to address the assembled young men, school children and women of the city. The audience is given in thousands, an obvious exaggeration, but its constitution indicates that it was subjected to a moral homily. Iamblichus describes it as extolling reverence for parents and the gods, as well as urging the cultivation of body and mind, and he is probably not far wrong.

Very soon Pythagoras is teaching once again. There is the usual uncertainty as to whether he earned his living by this means, but J. A. Philip (in *Pythagoras and the Early Pythagoreans*) thinks it unlikely and, on balance, it is more probable that he acquired land or engaged in trade. He may even have practised the craft of metal working learnt from his father. Croton and the cities under its influence are known to numismatists for their beautifully designed coinage. These are *incuse*, that is to say, instead of the edge-milling familiar in our own coins, theirs had embossed patterns, a very considerable achievement for the times. It has even been suggested that an interest in coinage as the abstract representation of goods and services may lie behind Pythagoras's preoccupation with number and number theory, though, as I hope to show, there are other possibilities.

In any event, as a teacher he enjoyed a renown in Croton that had eluded him in Samos. Isocrates speaks of the young flocking to study under his tuition and of their elders welcoming this. Here we seem to have the embryo of the so-called Pythagorean Brotherhood. In the sense of a community, sharing possessions, Philip doubts whether it ever existed. There is, to be sure, the tradition of the Spartan and Cretan 'syssition', the communal dining-hall and dormitory, which Pythagoras may have copied, though this does not, of course, necessarily imply permanent residence, far less the surrender of all personal possessions.

Claims that there were as many as 600 disciples all leading such a monastic life can safely be disregarded as springing from the over-enthusiasm of the author (in this case Iamblichus, citing Nicomachus, the son of Aristotle). We have, besides, reference to Pythagoras living in his own house with his wife and family, like any good bourgeois, while all of those identified by name with his movement lived so and participated in the life of the city.

Though we cannot overlook the possibility that some zealots may have chosen to live communally, it is difficult to reconcile this mode of life with the influence the Pythagoreans undoubtedly exercised over affairs. Communes usually comprise those who, for one reason or another, want to dissociate themselves from the world and neither wish nor are able to affect it. There is, on the other hand, no doubt that the Pythagoreans were a highly potent force in Croton, helping to shape policy through the political clubs that had sprung up in this as in all the city-states of Greece-in-Italy; indeed they appear to have been so active a coterie that they were spoken of as forming 'a city within the city' and of establishing an *aristokratia,* the word being used in its original and accurate sense of 'rule by the best'.

It could equally well have been applied to them in its more customary sense, for undoubtedly the Pythagoreans thought of themselves as an élite. This was to be expected of followers of Apollo, a god who, as I. M. Lewis writes, was only 'to be found in the best company', in contrast with his brother/alter ego Dionysus who did not seem to care who he mixed with.

The high-water mark in Pythagoras's political influence came when a quarrel broke out between Croton and its extremely prosperous neighbour, Sybaris. The seeds had been sown in the war with Locri, for having lost territory by their defeat, the Crotoniates were seeking to make it good by stealthy annexations of tracts across the Sybarite border, a proceeding bound to end in the exasperation of the loser.

However, the immediate cause was both different and, seemingly, more trivial. Some time before, the demagogue Telys had established himself as tyrant of Sybaris and in a populist move had persuaded his followers to seize the property of five hundred of its richest citizens, who were then banished. The dispossessed magnates presented themselves at the gates of Croton and begged sanctuary. Its assembly deliberated – hesitated – but admitted them, apparently because of the pleading of Pythagoras. Then Telys changed his mind and demanded their return, threatening war if this was not done. Again the Crotoniates deliberated and, mindful of their recent abasement at the hands of the Locrians, would probably have given in, but for another stiff dose of rhetoric from Pythagoras.

His sympathy for the refugees is, perhaps, no more than is to be expected. They came from the same class as himself – the mercantile aristocracy. Telys was, in his view, just another usurper, like Polycrates. But his antipathy to the Sybarites may have had a deeper cause: their love of luxury – the name has of course become a synonym for it. Among the richest of all the commercial cities of the entire Greek world, it had abandoned itself to the pursuit of pleasure. Cooks who produced new dishes were granted patent-rights; those who sold purple dye or such delicacies as eel were given generous tax concessions or so, at least, the satirists claimed, probably not without some foundation.

Not only must this have damned them in the eyes of the apostle of 'nothing in excess', it must have been convincing evidence they were too far gone down the road to perdition to be capable of defending themselves against those imbued with his sterner ideals.

So it proved. When Telys, as good as his word, marched against Croton, he was met by its army, commanded by Milo, a wrestler of international renown, prospective son-in-law of the physician Democedes and a prominent Pythagorean. The Sybarites, in spite of a three to one superiority in numbers, were routed and their city captured.

* * * * *

The Pythagoreans' political ascendancy seems to have continued unchallenged down to about the turn of the century. However, as is the invariable case with exclusive coteries, and especially with one so impenetrably secretive, they were never short of enemies. Among them was the old landed aristocracy, who saw them as upstarts with an intolerable air of superiority. Matters appear to have come to a head when one of them, Kylon, encouraged revolt. Some say he was aggrieved at having been refused membership on the grounds of his own doubtful moral character, others that he represented only one jaw of what was, effectively, a pincer attack. Its complement came from a local politician with populist ideas, an incipient tyrant, who charged the Pythagoreans with a reactionary opposition to reform. Whatever the truth, angry mobs roamed the city streets, burning, looting and killing, making a special target of the Pythagoreans.

Pythagoras is said to have left the city before these distressing events, having been prophetically warned of their imminence. If this is so it is surely strange that he left his followers to their fate. As if to acquit him of the charge, we are told by some writers that at the time he was actually in Delos, nursing the dying Pherecydes, his old teacher. This may well be true, though whether this coincided with the Kylonian uprising or was earlier has never been established.

So far at odds are the sources that not even a tentative chronology of events is possible. For example, was the Kylonian revolt combined with a second, populist one, or were the two actually separate occurrences? If so, how long elapsed between them? Were they of brief duration or did they smoulder on? Most of all, did Pythagoras return to Croton from Delos? Some witnesses affirm that he did and that the war with Sybaris and the revolts took place after his return. In one account (accepted by Guthrie) he fled the prowling mobs and, in search of sanctuary, turned to the city's erstwhile enemies, the Locrians. They sent a deputation to meet him at their border, paid fulsome tribute to his reputation and ability, but, none the less, begged him to look elsewhere. They were quite content with things as they were in their city.

He is said to have then gone to another Italian city, Metapontum, where, apparently still pursued by enemies, he took refuge in the Temple of the Muses – who were, of course, linked with Apollo – and there he died of starvation. That his death was self-induced is unlikely, since he prohibited suicide.

In another version, however, he was killed by the rebels when he refused to cross a field of beans to make good his escape. As to his age at death, Iamblichus says he was nearly a hundred. This is obvious idealizing: prophets were expected to be long-lived and, besides, Pythagoras was supposed to have considerable medical skill and to maintain a careful diet. It is far more likely that he was in his seventies, an age consistent with the various dates and time scales available to us, which puts his death at about the year 500 BC.

5. Genesis of the Daimon

In the foregoing brief outline of the life of Pythagoras it has, of course, been impossible to stick rigidly to incontrovertible fact because, as is so often the case with the ancient world, this is so sparse it could be contained in a sentence or two. Even the facts we have are not indisputable. Instead I have presented the various versions given by those whose credentials are most reliable, wherever possible indicating why, in my opinion, one is to be preferred over another.

We have already seen that, besides being the teacher of a philosophical system, Pythagoras was regarded as a prophet. In the Renaissance the title of Magus was freely applied to him. This is no more than a euphemism for 'magician' and in the Greek, from which it comes, signified precisely that. It was used in fifteenth-century Europe because magic had overtones of witchcraft and the conjuration of evil spirits, which not only set it beyond the pale of intellectual respectability, but could also call down the wrath of the Church. It was to prove one of the disappointments of the Renaissance that the revolution in religious beliefs it had wrought was not to be extended to greater tolerance in the direction of occultism. In this respect, as in so many others, the reformed Church proved as obdurate as the unreformed.

The mark of the magician was his special relationship with the universal – the elemental – forces, which enabled him to communicate, even unite himself, with them. He felt, saw, heard things intangible, invisible and inaudible to others. He could address animal creation and, through this, possessed power over it.

Such abilities were certainly comprehended in the title *daimon* attached to Pythagoras, one intended to express the favour shown him by Apollo whose mark he bore as his famous 'golden thigh'.

There are certain signs by which, traditionally, those chosen by destiny have been recognized by their fellows. Invariably, their coming into the world is accompanied by some marvel. The birth of the Buddha was foretold by his mother's dream in which the sacred white elephant touched her left side with a lotus; the birth of Christ, offspring of the Holy Spirit, was announced by the angel Gabriel. In the case of Pythagoras, we find his mother, Parthenis, the virgin, becoming pregnant by the intervention of Apollo.

Such beings are expected to refine innate gifts through a long and arduous period of training at the hands of those with arcane and esoteric knowledge. So we have Pythagoras setting off on his travels, their twenty-year duration corresponding with the twenty-year training period of the Druids, the Brahmins or the Magi.

Training is always crowned by a time of lonely contemplation. It was through this that the Buddha achieved Enlightenment, while Christ had his forty days in the wilderness. The experience is one of hunger, thirst and terrifying hallucinations, the gradual mergence with the surrounding forces. It culminates in a ritualized death and rebirth, events symbolized in the Christian baptism and the Jewish circumcision. In the case of Pythagoras, the period of contemplation took place in Crete, where he was initiated into the secret rites of Idaean Zeus.

Magical Powers

The true magician proves his credentials by miracle working and in this, too, Pythagoras fulfils expectation. The available description of his supposed acts are by no means derived solely from the more gullible sources. They are mentioned by Aristotle, though, as his work on Pythagoras is lost, one cannot tell with what degree of scepticism.

It is said that once, when crossing a river, the *genus loci* was heard to call, 'Hail, Pythagoras'. On another occasion, when a venomous snake crossed his path, he was said to have picked it up and killed it with a bite. Not all his dealings with the animal kingdom were so fatal to their recipients. When the Sybarites caught a snake, he let it go free. In Croton, he formed such a close relationship with an eagle that the creature came at his bidding and let him stroke its head. He whispered in the ear of a bull about to eat in a field of beans and it obediently turned away. On another occasion, he instructed a bear not to eat meat and it forthwith abandoned its deplorable habit.

These last two stories naturally also bear a moral message consistent with Pythagorean teaching, as meat and bean eating were both tabooed. They have also been interpreted as indicating that Pythagoras possessed hypnotic skill. Heroes able to entrance animals abound in myth and folk-legend worldwide and the attribution of this ability to Pythagoras would help to strengthen the view of him as the possessor of occult powers.

At the same time, the Pythagorean miracles also had a deeper allegorical meaning. Water was regarded as a living thing and legends in which it speaks or is the agent of wonders are particularly common among the Indo-Europeans. Many of the Celtic gods were associated with water and, according to Herodotus, the Magi sacrificed white horses to their river gods.

The snake slaying also belongs to ancient myth. A silver cauldron of undoubted Celtic provenance found in Denmark, shows on one of its panels a god grasping a snake in his left hand as if strangling it. And Apollo, we can hardly forget, took possession of the oracular shrine of Gaia after destroying the Python, while for Orpheus the snake was the creature that killed his wife, Eurydike.

As the snake is a dweller in the underworld, the eagle is a creature of the heavens and, being the bird which could fly higher than any other, was especially sacred to the sky-god, Zeus, who frequently employed it as his messenger. Again the idea is not exclusively Greek. It occurs in Scandinavia and the Celtic lands. Geoffrey of Monmouth refers to an island in Loch Lomond where there were sixty eagles' eyries, to which they flocked 'together each year and foretold any prodigious event which was about to occur in the kingdom'.

The bull is, of course, the animal associated with Dionysus as the creature he entered during his festivities and through which his worshippers, by eating its raw flesh, absorbed his divinity. It is also one of the manifestations of the same god in the Orphic Rhapsodies.

The bear, more of a rarity in Greek mythology, is, none the less, connected with Apollo through his sister, Artemis, whose name contains the bear-element, Art-. In a fit of jealous pique she turned her nymph Kallisto into a bear and the young girls who served in her temple at Athens were rather charmingly called 'the little bears'. Although principally identified with the moon, this seems also to connect her with the constellation of the Little Bear (Ursa Minor), which is not improbable since there are a number of similar links between her brother and the Great Bear (Ursa Major), especially in his Hyperborean manifestation.

As evidence that Pythagoras was indeed a *daimon* to his own age, as he was a magus to later ones, the stories of his mastery of animals serve the dual function of demonstrating a specific magical gift as well as his close relationship with the brother and sister gods. At the same time, other abilities of an occult nature were attributed to him. He cast horoscopes, an art he was said to have been taught by Anaximander, supposedly the first Greek to do so. However, it is equally probable he learnt it on his travels in the east. The Magi and Babylonian priests were pre-eminent in this field and the latter, in particular, are generally believed to have been the inventors of the zodiac, giving the various constellations the names we still use.

It was also said of Pythagoras that he possessed powers like those of Orpheus, who could move rocks by mental effort alone or by the effect of his music. This is sometimes interpreted as psychokinesis, though the examples we have are quite different from such phenomena as now recognized and it is more likely they were intended as proofs of the doctrine of 'like is known to like'; in other words, that all nature was informed by a single unifying principle which certain gifted beings were able to influence. Thales, we know, conducted experiments with lodestone and amber, both possessing the ability to attract other bodies to them, to demonstrate this. Lodestone and amber also have links with Apollo; the first because of its power to indicate north, the god's homeland, and the second because of its golden colour and its seemingly mysterious character as 'the stone that burned', all fire being thought to derive from the sun. In consequence, amber was often called 'the tears of Apollo'. The inhabitants of the shores of the Baltic, where amber is found, were said to have a special affinity for Apollo, and Tacitus scornfully mentions their superstitious belief that when he rose from the waves in the morning, his head crowned in rays, they could actually hear the sound he made.

Two further attributes of Pythagoras need to be considered. One is his belief in the transmigration of the soul. In spite of Herodotus, the belief did not exist among the Egyptians or the Persians. On these grounds, it might seem as if Pythagoras could have derived it from the Celtic Druids. The Druidic belief took two forms. In its later and more refined version, it was restricted to certain heroes who, after death, did not enter another body but 'slept' until some great crisis in their people's affairs should summon them from the tomb. This idea may have been taken from the Scythians, who influenced the Celts in so many ways and who buried their chieftains in chariots complete with horse, armour and weapons as if in preparation for their return.

The earlier and more primitive form of the belief seems to have predated the discovery of the link between intercourse and conception. A woman became pregnant, it was apparently believed, when a spirit, unhoused by death, entered her body, adopting, in order to bring this about, all manner of subterfuges – disguising itself as a fly that was accidentally swallowed in a drink, or taking on the form of a piece of food.

Belief in the wandering spirits of the dead searching for new homes, what used to be called animism, is still to be found and was no doubt widespread at earlier periods in human history. It may well have been that in Greece such ideas were among those transformed and systematized by the reforming zeal of Orpheus, just as in India it was transformed first by Hinduism and then Buddhism. Thus Orphism, rather than Druidism, is the most likely source of the Pythagorean teaching.

The belief in transmigration is not, of course, limited to esoteric or occult systems, though it is often to be found in such contexts. We are, however, justified in concluding that the descriptions of the previous existences of Pythagoras were intended to reinforce the claim he was a *daimon*.

Like Apollonius of Tyana, he was supposed to be anamnesic, in other words, able to recall all his previous lives. Heraclides of Ponticus (*c.* 390 BC) says the gift was granted to an ancestor in return for a favour he had once performed for the god Hermes. The first incarnation of Pythagoras was as Aethalides, the next as the Homeric hero Euphorbus, wounded by Menelaus at Troy, and able to recall his intervening existences as plants and animals, and even his sojourns in the underworld between lives. Next he was Hermotimus of Klazomenai, who proved his previous life as Euphorbus by identifying the rotting shield of Menelaus in the Temple of Apollo at Brachidae. Then he became the Delian fisherman Pyrrhus. Finally, he was reborn in the shape of Pythagoras.

One has to compare this with Plato's account of the destiny of the soul. Here, before leaving the Other World to rejoin that of the living, each soul is given a draught of the Waters of Oblivion, which is the reason why we have only sketchy memories of previous existences. Before the ninth and final incarnation the potion of Lethe Water is omitted so that the memory of the past remains. The newborn then returns as a member of one of the more exalted callings: a priest, a poet, or – significantly – a philosopher. Hence, Pythagoras appears to be in his final incarnation and destined to enter full divinity after death. It may be this, rather than Heraclides's story of the reward of Hermes, that accounts for his ability to remember his past incarnations.

The second attribute that must be discussed is Pythagoras's supposed ability to quit his body and travel freely as a disembodied spirit, a gift associated with shamanism. According to Aristotle, he was seen in two places at the same time; but these journeys did not only take him through the physical world. He also descended to the Kingdom of Hades; that is to say, he made precisely the same journey as that of Orpheus in his attempt to rescue the dead Eurydike.

The name Pythagoras is not the only one with which such

stories have been associated. Herodotus recalls that Aristeas of Proconnesus, inspired by Apollo, decided to leave his native island in the Sea of Marmara and go off in search of the Hyperboreans. He met with no more success than his predecessors, but apears to have reached Scythian lands where he was initiated into the practices of the Enarees, an élite very similar to the Druids.

Herodotus goes on to relate how, years later, Aristeas, visiting a shop in his home town, apparently fell dead. The alarmed shopkeeper at once closed his doors and went to break the news to the dead man's family. While on his way he met a visitor from the neighbouring city of Cyzicus. He imparted the staggering news that he had just seen and talked to Aristeas there. The shopkeeper, obviously sceptical, continued on his mission, but when the family reached the shop to fetch the body, it had gone. Seven years after this, Aristeas reappeared, only to vanish again.

His final epiphany was in Metapontum in Southern Italy, whose citizens he instructed to erect an altar in honour of Apollo with a statue of himself beside it. After consultation with the Delphic Oracle, this was done and – so Herodotus declares – the statues were still standing in his own lifetime.

A similar ability to leave his body was attributed to one of the early incarnations of Pythagoras, Hermotimus of Klazomenai. He was said to travel great distances and bring back 'much mantic lore and knowledge of the future' from such journeys. He perished when enemies, coming upon his body while his soul was elsewhere, decided he was dead and put it on the funeral pyre.

These descriptions bring to mind mediumistic trance, for here too contact is said to be made with the Other World. Was Pythagoras a psychic medium? There is abundant evidence to suggest that if he was not, there were those who were anxious to present him so. It is also quite plain that the gift of trance, like those of divination and prophecy, were believed to be endowed by the Hyperborean Apollo, since not only Pythagoras but also Aristeas and Hermotimus are linked with him.

Apart from his shamanistic ability to appear in two places at the same time and his similarly shamanistic visits to the Other World, we also have, linked with Pythagoras, the shadowy figure of Abaris. He is described as a Hyperborean; he comes to Pythagoras on the instruction of Apollo and recognizes him at once by his golden thigh. Even more instructive, however, is that Abaris possesses a golden arrow that enables him to travel invisibly wherever he chooses. This must be the projectile that Apollo looses from his own golden bow. Travel by means of magic arrows is a metaphor frequently used by the shamans for their spirit-journeys and reminds one of the broomstick flights of the European witches. It is still practised among the shamans of the Altaic regions of Siberia and, as Geoffrey Ashe explains, the word *Altai* actually means 'golden', while Herodotus mentions the legend of a gold-bearing mountain guarded by griffins, which Aristeas's Scythian hosts described to him. One can hazard the opinion that Abaris was himself a psychic medium and if he did not actually help Pythagoras develop his talents, he at least recognized him as one like himself, Hermotimus and Aristeas who enjoyed the special regard of Apollo.

But one can go still further and suggest that the Greek philosopher of the time looked upon the cultivation of psychic gifts as an essential part of his task, one that was almost the hallmark of his calling; and, since the Greek word *ekstasis,* the root of our own 'ecstasy', actually meant 'to leave the body', one may suspect that the ability to do so was taken for granted. In Plato's *Phaedo*, Socrates passes the time before he is due to take his own life in trying to convince his friends that there is no reason to fear death. In one passage which has bedevilled translators, as it has mystified commentators, he speaks of the soul of the philosopher seeking truth 'all by itself' by abandoning the body and implies that death will simply make this transitory state a permanent one. It will be a final release from the bondage of the physical. Guthrie comments that this suggests that perhaps there are means of attaining knowledge other than the normally accepted ones and it is surely suggestive that Socrates's visitors included two Thebans said to have studied with Philolaus, an original Pythagorean.

There is another clue to Pythagoras's nature: his alleged habit of taking *kykeon*. Porphyry's recipe may or may not be the true one, for it is generally accepted that it was a drug of the type pharmacologically classified as an 'ego-suppressant', a hallucinogen producing in the taker the sensation that he is no longer an isolated entity, but capable of such expansion that he can merge with all his surroundings, become part of the entire universe or travel freely from the depths of the oceans to the highest stars.

It is noteworthy that the sensation of mergence with one's surroundings can also be produced by prolonged exposure to certain drum rhythms: this is a characteristic of Voodoo ceremonies. One wonders whether the Pythagorean preoccupation with music was not in part due to its ability to induce such feelings, percussion playing an important part in Greek music.

We also know that the taking of hallucinogens was widely practised. Besides the Persian *haoma*, the Brahmins had their milky white *soma* for ritual purposes. There is also evidence that the 'mead' which Odin, whose designations include that of 'The Great Shaman', stole from Asgard and gave to mankind was not at all the comparatively innocuous beverage made from fermented honey but a much more potent brew, and that something similar was used by the Druids. In any case, there are numerous examples of the use of ritual drugs, among them those of the Aztecs, said to be derived from the seeds of Morning Glory, as well as the button-like fruit of the peyote cactus, the source of mescalin, used in Central America. Finally, there is the red-capped toadstool, Fly Agaric, chewed by the northern European shamans and said to give the illusion of flying.

6. 'All Things Are Number'

The intriguing problem in any discussion of the personality of Pythagoras and the influences that came to bear on him is: what is the source of his obsession with number and numerical relations? Everything, he declared, is assimilated to number. It is the starting point for his theorizing in the realms of morality as well as in those of astronomy and music, for number was the 'cause of gods and daimones'.

As the numbers that 'caused' gods and daimones were plainly quite different from those in normal, practical, everyday use, what did he mean? Aristotle advances four tentative interpretations: that all things owed their existence to the imitation or representation of number; that the elements of number and the elements of things are the same; that things were actually composed of numbers. Eurytus, one of the original disciples, seems to be giving his support to the last when he fixes the number of each entity by forming its outline from pebbles. In this way the total needed to make the figure of, say, a man was the number of mankind in general.

On this Aristotle pours scorn. As he points out, if this is the case, then many things will turn out to be the same, since more than one can be shaped out of the same number of pebbles. His fourth suggestion is that perhaps numbers stood for what we might call 'formulae', as, for example, in an equation. In his time it was believed that everything in existence was composed of the four basic elements, earth, air, fire and water, mixed in certain proportions. Bone, for example, comprised three parts of fire and two parts earth. Numbers, then, might represent the amounts of these constituents in any particular entity.

But, as he points out, there is an objection to this, too. While it may be possible to describe concrete objects in this way, what of qualities such as hot, cold, ugly or beautiful? Yet, undoubtedly, the Pythagoreans went even further and apportioned numbers to abstracts. Opportunity was seven, which, it was argued, came from the fact that it played a predominant role in human life. The infant can be born at seven months, begins cutting teeth after another seven, reaches puberty at about the second period of seven years and grows a beard at the third.

On the same scale, justice is four (2×2); masculinity, an odd number; femininity, an even one, so that the marriage becomes five, being the union of the first even and first odd numbers.

How did Pythagoras come by these ideas? It has been suggested that they may have developed from his involvement in commerce and a merchant's quantitative interest in goods, a view supported by Aristoxenus, a musicologist, personal friend of several of the early Pythagoreans and the author of a lost treatise on the movement. Others, as we have seen, believe it arose from the contemplation of coinage as the abstract representation of value. But many other possibilities have been advanced.

Number and mathematics have the character of immutable truths. Two multiplied by two is always four. One, whether divided or multipled, even when its square root is extracted, remains steadfastly, and perhaps in some ways miraculously, one. Thus, numbers have about them the attributes of absolutes and of the gods themselves, which may be why number and especially one, the Sacred Monad, played such an important role in Orphism.

Besides this, in his travels, Pythagoras probably encountered either the Babylonian Chaldeans or the Persian Magi, both of whom, as well as being mathematicians, also practised numerology.

Guthrie, on the other hand, believes he was profoundly affected by the realization of the mathematical relations underlying the musical octave. Pythagoras and his followers gave music an exceptionally high place in their activities. It spoke to the soul, inducing changes of mood. This, again, would be consistent with Orphism, founded by a musician and singer who, in the opinion of Pausanias (*c.* second century AD), 'surpassed those who went before him'. In one well-known legend, he was said to have charmed the birds and animals with his melodies, and in another to have used them to protect the Argonauts from the fatal song of the Sirens. Apollo, his tutelary god, was also a master musician, having been given the first lyre by Hermes. It is, therefore, not surprising to find Pythagoras described as being similarly gifted: he even used his music, as did Orpheus and Apollo, to cure the sick of body or mind.

With their interest in music rivalled only by their fascination with number, one might have expected the Pythagoreans to have attempted to combine the two, and indeed Pythagoras has been hailed as the discoverer of the fact that the A-string of the seven-string lyre had to be half the length of the G-string, a ratio of 2:1, to give a full octave, while the intervening strings were related to one another in proportions of 3:2, 4:3 and so on. This means that all were derived from the number series 1, 2, 3, 4, adding up to ten, a number which the Pythagoreans regarded as possessing very special attributes.

Whether or not Pythagoras actually was the discoverer is another question. According to a story circulating soon after his lifetime, he had stumbled upon the idea after listening to the notes struck by blacksmiths' hammers of different weights as they hit the anvil. In another story he was said to have experimented with the tension on a string by increasing the weight suspended from it. In fact neither the weight of a hammer nor increasing the weight at the end of a string in any way alters the pitch of sound. Nor was this thought to be the case even in his own times. The belief then current was that it was a function of the velocity of movement: as speed increased so the pitch altered.

Guthrie observes that the Greek *lyra* and *kithara* had strings of equal length and that modulation was achieved by the player stopping them at various points. He takes this as evidence that the mathematics involved in their design were unknown before Pythagoras. However, a stone carving of a musician found in

Keros and dated to between 2800–2200 BC shows a triangular-framed instrument. This is the shape that would be necessary if strings of graduated length were used and it is this very shape which is one of the things that distinguishes the harp from the lyre. The harp was known in Mesopotamia from as early as 3000 BC and it is likely to have been in use in the Celtic world in Pythagoras's lifetime. As an accomplished musician himself, it seems unlikely he knew nothing of it or of its design.

The Golden Section

Important as the musical octave may have been, it seems to me more likely that it was one factor in persuading the Pythagoreans of the absolute primacy of number, rather than the initial cause of it. And I also believe that there is other evidence at least supportive of their belief and which scholars have so far ignored.

The Greek word *harmonia* only gradually acquired an exclusively musical connotation. It originally signified the way in which the components of the whole fitted together, as, for example, the way in which the legs and back of a chair fitted to the seat. It was also sometimes used to mean the joints themselves or their securing pegs (*armos* is, in fact, the modern Greek word for a joint). But the parts of a chair would fit together so it fulfilled its intended function only when care was taken over its dimensions. Its design could, therefore, be rendered, as every carpenter knows, in terms of the dimension of its parts – that is to say, by numbers. The Pythagoreans looked to such practical activities as carpentery for many of their illustrations, using, for example, the carpenter's square in much of their arithmetical theorizing.

However, dimension and measurement become even more critical when, instead of static objects, one considers those intended to move, such as spoked wheels. Unless each part is measured and shaped to rigid tolerances, the wheels will not be circular. Equally important, wheels are not normally used singly, but in pairs and both must be of exactly the same size.

As the function of the wheel is to move, so the universe itself displays movement in all its parts, from the planets themselves through the rhythm of tides to the movement of animals, or the infinitely slow movements of growing plants. This would suggest that as dimension ruled in the realm of human artefacts, it also ruled the rest of creation, the Cosmos. It follows that one of the objects of the Pythagorean quest for number could be said to discover universal dimensions.

But there is more to dimension than pure function. To return to the example of the chair: besides utility, it is also required to be pleasing to the eye. It had to have proportion, a matter of particular importance to the Greeks, unsurpassed in their use of it. They derived it from the so-called Golden Section, to be found by dividing a line into two unequal parts so that the lesser part will be in the same proportion to the greater as greater to the whole. For example, if a line of 8 units is divided at 5 units, thus leaving three, then 5:8 is roughly in the same proportion as 3:5.

Though the accurate computation of Golden Sections involves comparatively complex mathematics, there is a simple and reliable method of finding it that is known and used by artists down to the present day. The side of any square is related to its diagonal in the proportions of the Golden Section. For example, if a diagonal is drawn through a square 5×5 it will be found that this is approximately 8 units long (more exactly, 7.071067). If this figure is used as the width and 5 as the height, the resulting figure is said to be a Golden Rectangle.

The importance the Greeks attached to the Golden Section and the Golden Rectangle is manifest in countless of their works of art, among them the Parthenon.

Nor is it a mere artistic device, a useful way of arriving at satisfactory proportions in sculpture or architecture. It is the ratio to be found throughout nature in everything from the petals of a flower to the shapes of marine animacules. Even the whorls of the humble snail's shell owe their form to it. In the human body, to pick a few random examples, the hand is related to the arm, the head to the body, the features to the face, all in Golden Section proportions. Leonardo's famous drawing of a nude male with arms outstretched inscribed within a circle is no more than an attempt to give it dynamic representation. One need only contemplate one's own hand to find an illustration of it, for the top two joints of the index finger are related to the whole finger in precisely this proportion.

The first person to enunciate the Golden Section as a canon was the sculptor Polyclitus (fifth century BC) and it was certainly known to Plato, who borrowed freely from Pythagorean sources. Of his five so-called mathematical solids, two, the twenty-faced icosahedron and the twelve-faced dodecahedron, can only be constructed by the use of Golden Section proportions. The Golden Section was certainly in use well before Plato's time or that of Pythagoras. It was also known outside Greece, for it is to be found in Egyptian architecture, as in the tomb of Ramses IV (died 1160 BC).

It is hard to believe that the Pythagoreans can have been unaware of it and there are, indeed, indications that they were not. For one thing they were also interested in the five mathematical solids. As we have just seen, the Golden Section can be derived by drawing a diagonal through a square, thus dividing it into two right-angled triangles, which we know were a Pythagorean preoccupation. The last clue is that the calculation of the Golden Section involves the number five. Its mathematical formula is: square root of 5+1 over 2 equals 1.618. Five was one of the Pythagorean sacred numbers. The five-pointed star or pentagon, always associated with magic, and which also requires the proportions of the Golden Section for its construction, was one of their most important symbols.

Numbers and Letters

Familiarity with the mathematics of the Golden Section and the Golden Rectangle would obviously help to confirm the truth of the axiom that 'everything is assimilated to number'. But so, too, would the realization of the critical importance of accurate measurement in the construction of working parts. The Greeks had acquired their system of linear measurement, the *daktylos* and the *pous*, together with their alphabet from the Phoenicians, who had also provided the Hebrews with their alphabet. All three were trading peoples, an activity obviously calling for some form of numerical notation as a means of registering such things as the values of cargoes or the quantities of commodities into which they were divided. From at least the third century, the Greeks, instead of writing out numbers in full, took to using their initials, so that five, for instance, was represented by the first letter of the word *pente*. On the same basis, ten (*deka*) was represented by D, a hundred (*hekaton*) by H and a thousand (*murioi*) by M. Hence 50 was PD, 500 was PH and 5005 PMP.

The Phoenician system, which the Hebrews also took over, was more ingenious and more efficient. It used the letters of the alphabet as numerals on the following scheme: the first nine (those in our own alphabet from A to I) represented the digits; the next nine (J to R), the tens from 10 to 90. The remaining letters were the hundreds.

Because letters were doubling as numbers, any given word would, at the same time, also be a sequence of figures. For example (and for simplicity using our own Roman letters), the word 'dog' would also stand for the figures 4,60,7 (D=4, O=60, G=7). This obviously lent itself to semi-mystical speculation and to the development of forms of numerology. The Hebrews gave this the name of *gematria* and developed it into an occult art. Correspondences, often of the most recondite kind, were found between two words possessing the same numerical values, so, for example, as the word 'Sinai' was numerically equal to the Hebrew for 'ladder' it was supposed that there was a mystical connection between them.

The Greeks may not have copied the Phoenician system of numeration, but since Pythagoras himself was a merchant, he is likely to have known of it. In any case, gematric numerology was a recurrent theme in the literature of Persia.

In Hebrew mysticism, gematria forms a part of the Qabalah. This claims to be of great antiquity, but gematria itself did not begin to appear in rabbinic literature until a comparatively late date and may well have resulted from encounters between Jewish intellectuals and Greek Neoplatonists in Alexandria at about the beginning of the Christian era. It is particularly striking how closely some of the gematric numbers resemble those of the Pythagoreans. In both, for example, justice is an even number: in gematria, six; for the Pythagoreans, four. At the same time, love, health and harmony are five in both systems, and other parallels can be found.

The Pythagoreans of Renaissance times and later certainly took for granted that gematria was known and used by their classical predecessors and, indeed, produced a 'Christian

Qabalah' with its own gematria based on the Roman alphabet.

Indirectly, gematria takes one back to a time when magic and superstition dominated Greek thought, as it did that of other peoples. For the magician, the efficacy of his acts depends on knowing the true identities of the forces he is trying to invoke. Conversely, those who might have reason to fear the malevolence of a magician will go to considerable length to keep their identity secret from him. It was for this reason that in many cultures children were given two names, a public one by which they were known generally and a real, private one only guardedly divulged. The same principle was often applied to god-names, which were kept secret by their worshippers. A typical Celtic oath was, 'I swear by the gods by whom my people swear', obviating the need for identification.

Many of the god-names we have are, in fact, not names at all but descriptives. 'Zeus' simply means 'god'; 'Demeter', 'earth mother'. The nineteenth-century English Neoplatonist Thomas Taylor, who influenced the poets Blake and Shelley, associated the name of Apollo with the Orphic Sacred Monad, since in its Greek form of *Apollon* it means, he asserts, 'deprived of multitude'. He is perfectly right. *Pollon* means 'many' and the prefixed *a-* is a negative, as in *amnesic*, 'without memory'.

It was widely believed that once the true name of a god was known and he was addressed by it, he could refuse nothing. This view was certainly one shared by the Hebrews, who used gematria for this very purpose. Can it be that the Pythagoreans did likewise? The evidence that they called the Sacred Monad, 'Apollo' suggests they may have done. In most numerological systems, including the one ascribed to Pythagoras, the operator proceeds by adding together all the integers arising from his calculations until he can do so no longer; that is to say, when a single digit has been reached. The numerical values of the name Apollon, using the Greek alphabet, are 1, 70, 60, 20, 20, 60, 40, which total 271. When added again, this, of course, yields 10 – whose significance we shall later explore – while 1+0 equals one, the Sacred Monad. So extraordinary a coincidence was hardly one to have escaped the Pythagoreans.

PART TWO: THE TEACHINGS

7. The Pythagoreans

If the Pythagoreans did not form the kind of communistic monastic community some writers have portrayed, was there any kind of formal organization at all? There can, to my mind, be no doubt that a group of like-minded people did gather round the figure of the sage himself but, in its organization, it was probably more like something between a religious sect and a freemasonry than a commune. It certainly drew its membership from among those most prominent in city life.

As to meeting places, it could, of course, have been that they met in the open, in the *agora*, or at each other's homes. On the other hand, as men of substance, they may well have wished to give tangible expression to their beliefs by building a permanent centre, and this would accord with the references to Pythagorean meeting houses being burnt down during the Kylonian riots.

Like the members of any religious sect they were united by the objective of personal redemption. As this was to be achieved through adherence to a rigid set of beliefs and practices, 'values' as we might call them, it followed that they would see themselves as especially well qualified for leadership of their community. They would introduce a morality into public affairs, though perhaps it ought again to be stressed that this had more to do with ritual purity (which would have made them acceptable to the gods) than with duties to their fellows. It would, of course, have been stretching the credulity of an educated Greek to suggest that redemption was for all sorts and conditions of men. Immortality was, by definition, the gift of the gods and could not, therefore, be available to *hoi polloi,* the rude, ignorant and brutalized *Untermensch* who lived constantly on the borders of mutiny and frequently trespassed over it. The mere whiff of higher things might make them quite ungovernable. In any case, it was unlikely that the majority of their fellow-Crotoniates would adopt many of their practices, such as voluntarily relinquishing meat eating. As they were not on a mission of saving the world, it probably did not seem to matter to them very much. They would have viewed the various restrictions of Pythagoreanism as obligations laid upon them by their special position. All élites impose obligations and the willingness to accept them is, indeed, one of the emblems of membership.

Of their actual beliefs, four ground tenets can be isolated. They believed in the Orphic idea of an internal struggle between the Titanic, unruly side of the personality and the divine, Dionysiac side. They believed the Titanic part manifested itself in the physical with its temptations, and that the divine part was the soul which was immortal and went through a cycle of transmigrations until released by the accumulated merit of the individual. They believed in *Cosmos*, a word which incorporates within it the ideas of order and beauty, and implies the existence of a vital unifying thread running through the entire universe in all its diverse manifestations. While there is no reason to suppose that they abandoned orthodox Greek polytheism, they also believed in a superior divinity, the One. There is at least some evidence that they identified the One with the Hyperborean Apollo, although it is more probable that they regarded him as the intermediary between the supreme god and mankind.

Apollo had been accorded special devotion by Orpheus who, it was said, greeted the rising sun every morning by hymning its ruler; the Pythagoreans, we are told, did likewise. Like Pythagoras, too, Orpheus was 'the sent one' and 'the son of Apollo'. He is *Phoibos,* the Enlightener. It followed that knowing and carrying out the divine will as he expressed it was to be cultivated.

Taboos

Belief affects conduct and Socrates is probably glossing what was in origin Orphic and Pythagorean teaching when, in the *Phaedo,* he warns his listeners against the gratifications of the flesh and the risk of seeing nothing as real 'save that which is bodily, what can be touched and seen and eaten and made to serve sexual enjoyment'. Orphism and Pythagoreanism were as strongly imbued with hostility to the physical and the bodily as Gnosticism, Manicheeism and Christian heresies like Catharism, all of which may, in fact, have derived their teachings from the Pythagoreans. The soul was yoked to the body in punishment – presumably for the original outrage of the Titans in eating the child-god, Dionysus. The body was thus a prison or a tomb. In this life, it must be strictly and austerely disciplined, the ultimate aim being to free oneself from it. This is an idea that finds its apogee in Socrates's ability to make light of his imminent death for the very reason that it meant the liberation of his soul.

The belief in transmigration also entailed consequences for everyday living and attitudes. The strict Pythagorean prohibition on suicide no doubt arises from it, for it can have little point if it simply resulted in rebirth, though the prohibition also relates to the Homeric tenet that, since humans were the property of the gods, it was impious to circumvent one's fate by one's own hand.

We have already considered the taboo on meat eating. If it existed, as on balance it must have done in some form, it would have been based on the same doctrine – by eating meat, one was risking indulgence in cannibalism.

Similarly contradictory evidence to that which surrounds their meat eating is also to be found in the case of the Pythagoreans' alleged taboo on beans. Side by side with those who assure us that Pythagoras's abhorrence was such that he preferred death to crossing a field of them, we have others, like Aristoxenus, who tells us they were his favourite food on account of their 'purgative property'. This writer suggests that the belief in Pythagoras's proscription of beans came about through the mistaken interpretation of a line in an Orphic poem quoted by Empedocles: 'Thrice wretched, keep your hands from the beans'. Beans here apparently stood for the testicles and, if this is so, it would make sense of another Orphic verse cited by Graves (in *The White Goddess*) where it is implied that eating beans was equivalent to eating one's parents' heads. In ancient anatomy, it was believed that there was a connection between the head and the testicles so that, in colloquial speech, the one was used to signify the other. Thus a Roman father might exhort a son who had formed an undesirable liaison with a woman 'not to diminish his head with her', meaning not to indulge too freely in sexual activity.

For a taboo on beans we have a precedent. Herodotus claims that the Egyptians would not eat them 'because they imagine they are unclean'. The Egyptians, in fact, linked men and beans mythologically, as both were supposed to have been raised from the same primeval mud. Since the Roman *Flamen Dialis*, the ritual guardian of the Sacred Flame, was similarly interdicted, the conclusion might be that there was a general prohibition on beans throughout the ancient world.

Explanations for this are as multifarious as they are ingenious. The Egyptian myth makes the bean a sort of vegetative cousin to mankind, so eating them is another form of cannibalism. However, other reasons put forward are that they resembled the gates of Hades, that their stems were hollow and unjoined, that they had a 'flatulent tendency', that they looked like the female genitalia and that they smelt of semen. Porphyry and Pliny connect them with the souls of the dead and their return to earth, which has parallels in other cultures. The award for the most original explanation must surely go to Heraclides who claimed that a bean laid in a fresh grave and covered with dung will, in forty days, assume the likeness of a man.

Graves also points out an association of beans with witch cults, which may go further than anything else to explain the taboo. Although Apollo's sister, Artemis, was, as Hecate, the patroness of witches, it is likely that a superstitious, but male-oriented group like the Pythagoreans would have feared and detested witches as the representation of woman at her most threatening.

This same fear of witchcraft may help to explain some of the other Pythagorean taboos listed by Aristotle. These include not spitting or urinating on one's own nail-parings and hair-trimmings; smoothing out the body imprint and rolling up the bed clothes on rising; rubbing out the mark left by the pot in the ashes of a fire; not allowing swallows into the house.

Saliva, faeces, urine, nail-parings, blood or hair-trimmings, as bodily secretions, were all potential *materia magica,* which in the hands of the malevolent could be used for harmful spells. Smoothing out the body imprint on the bed and rolling up the clothes could have a similar prophylactic purpose, as such imprints, like shadows, could also serve malign ends. Rubbing out the mark of the pot could well have been to prevent magical contamination of the contents, while keeping swallows from the house could come from the age-old belief, still to be found, that these creatures are either transformed witches or their familiars, whose role was to act as spies.

Other taboos attributed to the Pythagoreans include: not picking up what has fallen from the table, not stirring the fire with a knife, not sitting on a bushel measure, touching the earth when it thunders, not wearing a ring. Attempts have been made to see these as examples of proverbial wisdom. For example, to sit on a bushel measure meant being smugly content with what one had already achieved instead of trying to scale fresh heights. Although Pythagoras had a reputation for concealing his teachings in metaphor, superstition again offers a more tenable explanation – the injunction to touch the earth when it thunders is a clear example. Such small propitiatory rites of this kind are known to the folklore of most peoples.

The Pythagorean ban on wearing a narrow or – some say – any ring obviously belongs to the realm of what Frazer, in the *The Golden Bough,* calls 'sympathetic magic', the kind of magic that assumes things can act upon one another even at great distances. Guthrie adds to this another taboo against wearing anything with knots. Both restrictions were also placed on the *Flamen Dialis* and are of such antiquity as to have been absorbed into the human psyche, as can be seen by the enormous number of idioms involving knots and binding, to say nothing of the words derived from them. Eliade devotes an entire essay in his *Images and Symbols* to the theme of knots and the 'god who binds'. Those who are so bound are the transgressors against the laws of ritual purity and the ability to bind is a characteristic frequently attributed to the lords of the underworld, of which Hades is the Greek exemplar. It is also true that, in many languages, the word for 'bewitchment' is a cognate of 'tying'.

Lastly, we have that group of taboos that surround birth and death. In Euripides's *Cretans*, a character says, 'Clothed in raiment of white, I shun the births of men nor touch the affairs of the dead and keep myself from eating food which has life.' The last line hints at Orphism and it is likely that the Pythagoreans had similar prohibitions. That the dead are polluting is a widely held belief, but the same is true for many aspects of birth, so that in many societies the midwife was shunned as a witch and thought to possess her powers. However, the reference to 'white raiment' brings to mind Pliny's description of the mistletoe-gathering rite among the Druids, which, he tells us, culminated in the sacrifice of a white bull – coincidentally, the animal associated with both Crete and, in the Orphic Rhapsodies, with Dionysus.

As to the Pythagorean prohibition on burying their dead in wool, Herodotus refers to a similar Egyptian taboo, shared by the Orphics. Guthrie suggests that it may have come about because it was thought that stealing the wool of the sheep was equivalent to eating its meat. This sounds implausible for it would imply a ban on wool at all times, not just at death. As wool and skins provided the Greeks with much of their clothing materials it is difficult to see what they could have worn if deprived of these, especially in the frequently harsh winters.

While belief in reincarnation suggests itself as the reason for at least a partial assumption of vegetarianism among the Pythagoreans, and may also have been connected with their refusal to eat beans, there is a second possible reason. It is the belief in the kinship of life, that 'like is known to like', in the Pythagorean aphorism, which found its way into the philosophy of Plato. Interpreters of Pythagoras and Empedocles have, from earliest times, attributed to them the teaching that a Divine Breath united men with the gods at one extreme and with brute creation at the other. It was this Divine Breath that is the unifier of the Cosmos.

We are not at the point where a detailed examination of the concept of Cosmos would serve a useful object, though we may perhaps recall the longevity of the belief that 'like is known to like', which is the informing principle of Frazer's 'sympathetic magic'.

Here we must restrict ourselves to considering it as a determinant in the Pythagorean way of life. If man is intimately related to the universal and partakes in the Divine Breath, he has the obvious duty of discovering as much as he can about the environment in which he exists as the means of bringing himself into greater conformity with its underlying laws. In this sense, then, philosophy, the pursuit of wisdom, subserves what we should see as a religious aim. It was part of the redemptive process; a means of escaping the Wheel.

Physical Fitness

Besides the beliefs and practices so far discussed, it also seems to me likely that the Pythagoreans practised a cult of physical fitness. For one thing, it would have been part of the process by which the wayward physical body was brought under the command of the mind, but it also emerges from the host of other hints. First, there was the significance that sport was then assuming in Greek life. No city felt itself worthy of attention unless it staged a games in honour of its god, the most famous being the quadrennial Olympic Games, and Croton was a city that made a fetish of physical fitness. The Pythagorean Milo, commander of the victorious Crotoniate army in the war with Sybaris, was a wrestler of international renown, for instance.

Because of this Pythagorean involvement in sport, the supposed confusion between Pythagoras the philosopher and Pythagoras the trainer of athletes may have been due to more than a similarity of names. In one quotation, the sage distinguishes the diet necessary for an athlete in training from that for a philosopher: the one needed meat, the other should eschew it. On another occasion, when asked by Leon, tyrant of Phlius, to explain what he meant by the word 'philosopher', he used the analogy of the games. Some, he said, went to compete, others to trade. But most important of all were the spectators – those who observed and drew conclusions from their observations, as the philosopher observed and drew conclusions from the natural world.

Furthermore, we have the description of Iamblichus, who may have been using Aristoxenus as his source, of a typical Pythagorean day. This tells us how they spent a part of it caring for their bodies by running, wrestling, exercising with weights and shadow boxing.

Lastly, there is the example of Apollo himself who is always portrayed as the model of radiant, youthful fitness and whose own Pythian Games, held at the stadium at Delphi (the remains of which are still to be seen), were second only to those at Olympia.

What, then, were the qualifications for becoming a Pythagorean? Those modern writers who claim to see the community at Croton as an early democracy are not merely indulging in wishful thinking, they are displaying a woeful ignorance of Greek society of the time. Pythagoras himself came from what was, in effect, the upper class and the same was true of those of his followers known to history. Besides, his system was sufficiently complex to presuppose a degree of education on the part of his disciples.

Nor is there anything at all to show that Pythagoras was a model for William Wilberforce, setting free his slave, Zalmoxis, and sending him back to his native Thrace. Zalmoxis was, by general consent, exactly what Herodotus believed him to be, a Thracian god. The misapprehension probably arose from some over-patriotic Greek's attempt to explain the fact that both the Thracians and the Pythagoreans believed in reincarnation. As, in this view, Greece, like necessity, had to be the mother of invention, the doctrine of transmigration must have come from her and travelled eastward, rather than originating in Thrace and coming to Greece.

The prerequisite of education makes it extremely doubtful that there were ever women members, notwithstanding a comedy by the poet Alexis entitled *The Lady Pythagorean*. Save in exceptional cases, little attempt was made to educate Greek girls in anything beyond the domestic arts. The question remains a vexed one, however, with many distinguished commentators agreeing with Geoffrey Ashe (*The Ancient Wisdom*) that women were admitted.

It is certainly true that in Greek mythology and literature

women played a dynamic role. The goddess Athena, armed and casqued, crushes the giants of Sicily and throws herself into the fray at Troy. Antigone and Lysistrata, as the eponymous heroines of drama, show an independence of action as well as of mind. Though there is little reason to suppose such representations were a distortion, there was, none the less, a strict segregation of the sexes in the Greek household, with the wife remaining invisibly in the background when her husband entertained, for example.

Orpheus was always regarded as implacably anti-feminine and refused to initiate women. One reason for this was that they predominated in the orgiastic rites of Dionysus which he was endeavouring to extirpate. Apollo, too, seems to show a marked preference for the male, as the injunction to 'keep women under rule' in his temple shows, though legends of overt homosexuality as part of his worship are little more than sensational gossip.

If I am right in my belief that Pythagorean teachings included a stress on physical training, then this only increases the likelihood that women were excluded. Sporting activities were pursued in the nude. Exercise and training took place in *gymnasia*, a word which literally means a 'place of nakedness' (*gymnia* still means 'nudity' in Greek). In consequence, women were banned from the gymnasia, as they were from the games, including those at Olympia and those in honour of Apollo at Delphi.

* * * * *

Having established, at least in tentative form, some of the credentials for membership of the Pythagorean community, we can consider the next stage.

According to Iamblichus, of those who applied only a handful were accepted and had first to submit themselves to the kind of interrogation a young man seeking his first job might have to face, with questions about his motives, his family background and other interests; throughout this questioning his behaviour was minutely scrutinized. He was also subject to a three-year probationary period before final admission and had to swear a five-year oath of silence.

A number of witnesses speak of the Pythagoreans as being divided into two classes, the *akusmatiki* and the *mathematiki*, though there is considerable debate as to what these actually signified. In one passage in Iamblichus, the names seem to mark a differentiation in kind between those who adopted the tenets while living normal home lives and those who, surrendering all possessions, devoted their entire lives to study. In another passage, however, they are made to appear as grades of membership; aptitude in the first was rewarded by advancement to the second. Elsewhere, they are described as followers of the Pythagorean heretic Hippasus. The waters are further muddied by the introduction of another group to which the name *Pythagoristai* is applied. Gorman's suggestion is that they were a kind of order of Pythagoreans mendicant whose beggarly appearance led to the reputation gained by the sage's followers as the dropouts of the ancient world.

Once again we are faced with the impossibility of making a firm pronouncement. As Guthrie says, the existence of such groupings is 'inherently probable', though since three was a magic number to the Pythagoreans (as it was to the Druids and Brahmins), three rather than two divisions might be expected. Whether the *Pythagoristai* or, as some commentators hint, what were called the 'August' (*Sebastikoi*) were the third is uncertain. None the less, the word *akusmatiki* signifies 'hearers' – it is related to our own word 'acoustic' – and this seems to support Porphyry's description of them as those who were simple auditors of the master's teachings.

Etymological clues can also be applied to the word *mathematiki*. The restriction of mathematics to number-science is a late development (and one for which Pythagoras was probably indirectly responsible). In his own day, it means 'wisdom' or 'learning': in modern Greek *mathema* is still the word for 'lesson'. On this basis, the *mathematiki* would mean the learned ones, the adepts.

As we have seen, Pythagoras was credited with magical powers and it is likely that his followers were more than just a group of devoted disciples gathered round the feet of a teacher. There is little reason to doubt that activities of an esoteric and occult nature were pusued, though, in a system already notorious for its secrecy, only those who were totally trusted and had shown their ability would have participated in what must have been the most secret part of all.

Lifestyle

How did the Pythagoreans live? The schedule of daily activities offered to us by Iamblichus is so full that one is forced to wonder how it could ever have been adhered to. Rising at dawn, the first task of the conscientious Pythagorean was to set his mind in order for the coming day by solitary contemplative walks in the greenery of temple precinct and sacred grove. There was then a period devoted to study and 'the correction of moral qualities', followed by one of physical exercise. Then came a light communal breakfast of bread and honey, a particular point being made of abstention from wine during the day.

After breakfast, all would join in the discussion of affairs of state, a piece of information which, if accurate, confirms the view that Pythagoreans were drawn largely from the ruling class.

The last part of the day was given over to further walks, this time not alone but by 'two and threes'. Washing and religious observations, including sacrifice, preceded the evening meal, at which there was wine, barley cake, bread, roast, boiled and raw vegetables. Rather surprisingly, the author tells us that meat was served and, less frequently, fish. Both these statements, in any case at variance with the supposed vegetarianism of the Pythagoreans, are contradicted a little further on in the same excerpt, for after listening to a reading, the cups were filled for libations during which the assembly's leader recited an exhortation containing the words, 'Do not harm or destroy any cultivated thing, plant or tree, nor *any animal which is not harmful to mankind*' (my italics).

The whole programme is so similar to the rule of Christian monasticism as it was beginning to evolve that one suspects that this was the main source for much of this account and the fact that St Basil, one of the founding fathers of the monastic rule, was himself in Byzantium at the time of the accession of Julian may not be unconnected.

It may well have been that something akin to the monastic life had actually existed in the pagan world and that the

Pythagoreans' lifestyle was an example of it. Nevertheless, in view of the general anti-Christian bias of the writer, it seems more likely that he was chiefly concerned with proving that there was nothing original to be found in the new faith he so despised.

8. Cosmos and Limit

The structure of Pythagorean philosophy rests on two foundations.

The first is the concept of Cosmos. As we have seen, this untranslatable word, traditionally said to be of Pythagoras's own coining, embraces connotations of order, perfection and beauty; the interaction, one might say, of the parts in the whole as the various organs interact in the living creature. The Pythagorean Cosmos is, therefore, analogous to an enormous and highly complex clock, the master-work of a designer of supreme ingenuity.

This makes it the antithesis of chaos; it is organized and, for those of trained sensitivities, the marks of its organization, the impress of the designer, are everywhere to be found, as much in the tiniest seed as in the rotation of the heavenly bodies, even in the mathematics of the Golden Section whose forms permeate all nature.

Order, as an observable fact, presupposes limit, since a shape without predetermined limits is amorphous, literally without form.

The reverse of the Cosmos and order, the beginning of chaos, is therefore the unlimited and it is this polarity, limited-unlimited that is basic to Pythagorean teaching.

The unlimited is not only chaotic, it is deprived of time in the sense that it possesses none of the regular divisions of day and night, seasons and years by which Cosmic, that is to say ordered, time is marked. It is present in each individual as the Titanic part of our nature to be fought against and vanquished. It begins to take over the moment we leave the security of the monad. It is especially menacing in even numbers because they can be divided into exactly equal parts, leaving a potentially limitless void between them. Four can be split into two and two; five on the other hand, becomes 2+1+2 and so it is linked by the monad. The void between the two halves of even numbers was regarded as a womb, which is why for the Pythagorean even numbers are feminine and odd numbers masculine, the linking monad being the generative principle.

These pairs, limited/unlimited, odd/even, male/female, become the first in a list of Pythagorean antimonies, the others being one/plurality, right/left, at rest/moving, straight/curved, light/darkness, good/bad and square/oblong.

The second foundation, which, to some extent may be said to be the corollary of the first, is that everything within the Cosmos is 'assimilated to number'.

The Greek system of numerical notation might have been a convenient way of rendering whole numbers, but it did not lend itself to calculation. How, for example, was an accountant to add together THODT (=484) and PHPDP (=555)? The problem was solved by performing the actual calculations either using pebbles, possibly in a sand-tray, or by means of the Babylonian abacus, which had probably itself evolved from the sand-tray. When these were completed the answer was noted. This was undoubtedly the Pythagorean method since, for one thing, pebbles were in general use by the Greeks for calculating purposes, indeed the very word 'calculation' derives from their *kalkuli*, pebbles.

One of the first things to manifest itself would have been their tendency to form patterns and this was a matter of vast interest to the Pythagoreans. They noticed that three, for example, fell into a triangle, the first plane figure. If another three pebbles, making six, were added as a row along the bottom, another triangle was produced. The Pythagoreans were also interested in squares and observed that if any odd number was laid out so as to make a right angle or *gnomon* (a word which signified both the carpenter's square and the upright rod of a sundial), the

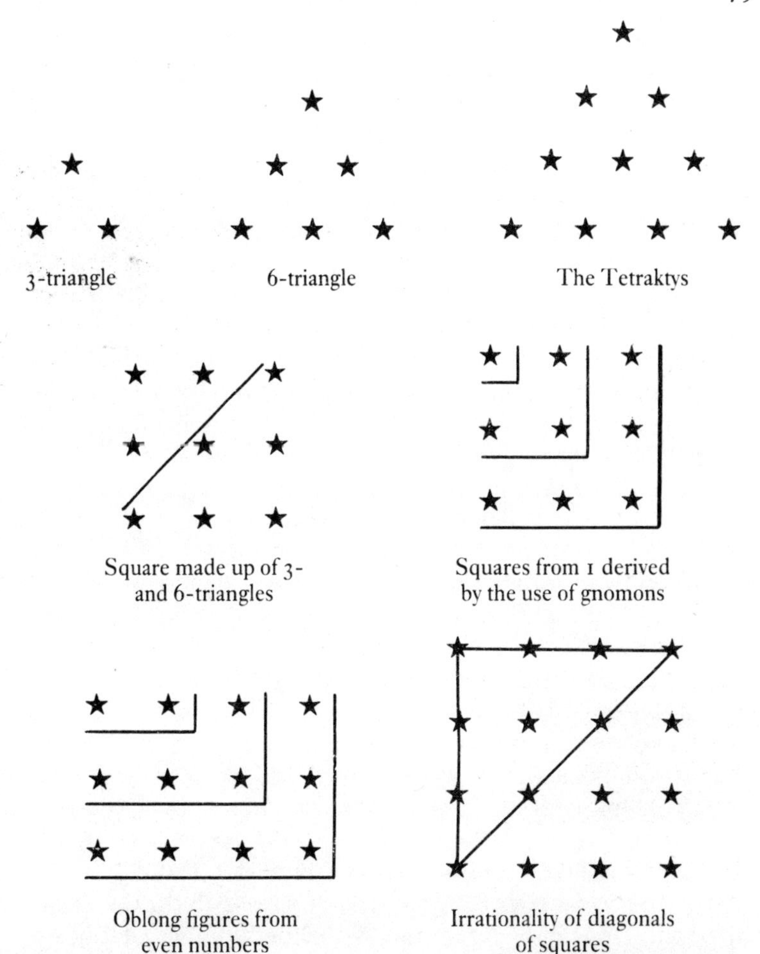

addition of further pebbles to fill the space in the open angle always produced a square number. Alternatively, square numbers could be generated by placing the gnomon round any lower figure starting from one. Thus, one pebble with the three others laid round it so as to form a right-angle makes the square number four (2×2).

The way in which odd numbers generated squares was contrasted with the tendency of even numbers to generate oblongs. The first oblong number is 2 and others are produced when a right-angle is placed round it in the sequence 6, 12, 20, 30 . . . It was for this reason that 'oblong' appears under the same heading as 'even', that of the 'unlimited'.

But this kind of experimentation with pebbles could also be deceptive. For example, if one makes a square of nine pebbles by laying them out in three rows of three and draws a diagonal through it, the diagonal appears to be three units long. However, if a graduated ruler is applied to it, it is found that this is not the case at all. In fact, the diagonal of the square is never a whole quantity; it is always one which has to be rendered in decimals or fractions.

For those to whom number was all, this was an obvious embarrassment, for they could hardly have anticipated unwieldy fractions manifesting themselves from so apparently logical a figure as the square. How the objection was answered no one knows, but one Pythagorean, Hippasus, is said to have been expelled from the movement, some say drowned, for pointing it out. As previously mentioned, however, it is said that he actually founded a body of dissidents, a species of Pythagorean heresy.

There was a second way in which square-figures could be generated. This was by drawing a diagonal through a pattern of pebbles formed into a square number, as for example, 16 (4×4). Two triangles then emerged, one of six and one of ten pebbles. Great significance was attached to the latter. For one thing it was the number of the fingers on the hands, and the Greek *delta*, the first letter of the word *deka* (10), is itself a triangle. Furthermore, the sequences of numbers making up the ten-triangle, namely, 1, 2, 3, 4, encompassed all the dimensions of space. One denoted position, two extension, three defined the simplest plane figure, and if a fourth pebble were supended over the others it made the simplest solid figure, the triangular-based pyramid or tetrad.

Given the name of the *Tetraktys* (Tetra=four, on account of its four levels) it became the sacred sigil of the Pythagoreans, who acknowledged the superhuman nature of their founder in an oath that included the words, 'By him who handed down to us the Tetraktys, fount and source of everlasting nature.'

But as we saw when discussing the numerological significance of the name of Apollo, the *Tetraktys* reduces numerologically to one. It thus becomes the Sacred Monad, which Thomas Taylor, in his *Theoretic Arithmetic of the Pythagoreans* (1816), extols in terms not very different from those which the Pythagoreans themselves might have employed. It is 'the principle and element of number'. When divided or multiplied by itself it remains unchanged. Added to an even number it converts it into an odd one; added to an odd number, it makes it even. In this way he sees it as corroborating Aristotle's assertion that it is both odd and even – male and female. 'It is,' he says, 'the first of all numbers that are in the natural series, and . . . deservedly acknowledged to be the source of all multitude, however extended it may be.'

That the Monad, reconciling within itself the opposed qualities of oddness and evenness and remaining unchanged whatever processes it was subjected to, should be raised to the status of a Platonic demiurge would be fully in accord with the central Orphic doctrine that everything comes from One and is resolved into it.

The contemplation of number led the Pythagoreans to many remarkable conclusions. One of them was the notion of deficient, superabundant and perfect number.

A deficient number is one whose divisors, including unity but excluding the number itself, when added together, total less than the original number. An example is 14, whose divisors are 7, 2, 1 which add up to 10. By contrast, a superabundant number is one whose divisors total more than the original number; for example, 12, whose divisors are 6, 4, 3, 2 and 1, which make 16.

Perfect numbers are those the sum of whose divisors exactly equal it, for example, 6 (3, 2 and 1) or 28 (14, 7, 4, 2, 1=28). They are of extremely rare occurrence. Only four perfect numbers were known to the ancient world, 6, 28, 496 and 8128. Another nineteen have since been discovered and it required the assistance of a computer to calculate five of these. This rarity led the Pythagoreans to compare perfect numbers with the virtues which were of equal rarity and required strenuous effort in their cultivation.

Perfect numbers possess two other qualities. All were triangular, that is to say capable of being formed into a triangle when laid out in pebbles; and all, with the exception 6, when treated numerologically, yielded first ten, then the monad: for example, if one takes 8128, then $8+1+2+8=19$; $1+9=10$; $1+0=1$.

The practice of deriving shape from number, so typically Pythagorean, led them beyond plane figures. The four of the *Tetraktys* was said to mark the limit points of the triangular-based pyramid, for example. They were also aware that while a number multiplied by itself yielded a square, if the resulting sum were again multiplied by itself a cubic figure emerged – one, that is to say, in three dimensions. The cube was one of the five 'mathematical' solids, together with the pyramid, the octahedron, the icosohedron and the 12-faced dodecahredon.

Obviously, all were accountable in terms of number, but they were also said to be the shapes of the elements. Thus, fire was a pyramid (there is a linguistic connection in Greek between the words 'pyramid' and 'fire'); earth was a cube; air, an octahedron; water, an icosohedron. The fifth solid, the dodecahedron (or, some witnesses say, the sphere), was the container into which the others fitted one into the other, like Chinese boxes. The fifth solid was the universal itself, the fifth element, the Divine Breath emanating from the One.

The Divine Breath

Just as the fifth solid was the egg from which the others were hatched, so the fifth element was the progenitor of the elements, beginning with fire; and it was out of their commixtures, in varying proportions, that all else sprang. For the Pythagoreans, therefore, the fifth element was the informing principle, the Cosmic substance, as for Thales it had been a hypothetical liquid, or for Anaximander a vapour.

From earliest times the Greeks appear to have believed in a soul, a psyche. It was, however, merely the agent of life, the prime mover, and at death was extinguished as a fire is extinguished by a pail of water. The Pythagoreans' Divine Breath, present in every living creature, was not only a second soul, it was one of quite different character. It was immortal in the true sense, for it passed from one existence to the next. It was in perpetual conflict with the physical, Titanic part of human nature and yearned always for reunion with the One.

It followed that the Cosmos, since it, too, was charged with the Divine Breath, was – like everything else – a living thing. The notion that the stars and planets possessed life was one generally accepted in the ancient world, which had no concept of the inanimate in the natural order, so that even minerals, such as gold, silver and iron, were thought to 'grow' much as plants or lichens. Gold, silver and iron mines, therefore, had to have what amounted to a 'closed season' in which they could replenish themselves under the influence of their governing planets.

The Divine Breath not only quickened the Cosmos, it also provided the medium in which it was suspended, drawing its own breath from it as the rest of creation breathed the coarser air of earth.

The Primal Fire and the Counter-Earth

What was the form of this totality, the Pythagorean Cosmos, which united earth and the heavens?

Commentators have frequently taken the primal fire, which was the first product of the Divine Breath, as referring to the sun. Hence it has been asserted that Pythagoras advanced the theory of a heliocentric universe, in opposition to the obtaining geocentric one, centuries before Copernicus and Galileo. To be sure, the Pythagorean universe was, like our metaphorical clock, in perfect balance, with each of the planets circling a fire which lay at the heart of the Cosmic sphere. While superficially this fire suggests the sun, it is clear from many sources, including Aristotle, that something quite different was intended. Aetius (third century AD) cites Philolaus as teaching that the visible sun was more or less in the nature of a mirror, reflecting heat and light which emanated from elsewhere. In this respect, sun and moon – which the Pythagoreans taught was inhabited by beings fairer and larger than those of earth – were similar.

The real fire, the hearth as well as the heart of the universe, was unseen by humanity because it lay directly under the uninhabited part of the earth and moved in synchronicity with it.

For exactly this reason, too, another Pythagorean construct, the counter-earth, was also unseen. As there were only nine observable planets (the sun and moon being included), Aristotle accused the Pythagoreans of inventing a tenth to prove the universality of the Tetraktys. There may be substance in the charge, but it is also possible that the hypothesis was intended to explain the more common occurrence of lunar than solar eclipses. According to this theory, it was the interpolation of the counter-earth that blocked out the moon's light.

However, we have available to us another interpretation of the theory of the counter-earth and the central fire. In this the former is actually identified with the moon, while the central fire is that lying at the core of the earth, itself the centre of the universe. As Guthrie says, this would be a 'natural inference from the observation of volcanoes and hot springs', and it is certainly consonant with the belief that the other elements came from fire; in other words, fire had woven around itself a protective mantle of the solid and liquid in the form of the earth's crust. It also accords with the belief, common to the Greeks, as to others that all life, vegetable and animal, originated within the earth, the Great Mother.

It was the motion of the heavenly bodies which brought about the divisions of night and day, the seasons and the circling year. In this way, timeless chaos has order and limit imposed upon it.

For the Pythagoreans, time was not an infinite continuum but, like the seasons of the year, cyclic. Each epoch came to an end and a new one began when sun, moon and planets returned to their starting points, calculated as coming about approximately every 10,000 years. Just as the terrestrial year was calculated in such a way as to harmonize the solar and lunar ones, this 10,000-year period was called the Great or Perfect Year. At each renewal human history recapitulated itself in its entirety, down to the smallest detail. The process was repeated ceaselessly; there was no theory of final cataclysm to bring an end to the Cosmos.

The Harmony of the Spheres

Irrespective of whether or not it was of Pythagoras's own discovery, the realization of the fact that the musical interval depended on the numbers of the *Tetraktys*, simultaneously demonstrating both the Law of Limit and the primacy of number, must have appeared as startling confirmation of his teachings. But it brought with it another and seemingly even more astonishing realization. The heavenly bodies must be rotating at enormous speeds. Since the emission of sound was related to the velocity of movement, it must follow that these bodies produced sound. Pythagoras's calculations showed that the planetary orbits were separated from one another by distances proportional to the numbers of the *Tetraktys*. This being so, they could only be emitting harmonious sounds. Thus, the theory of the Harmony of Spheres, certainly a Pythagorean invention, was born.

Pythagoras even claimed that he could hear those harmonies, and he was not the only one to do so. From his own lifetime, down to that in which the discovery of the true nature of sound disproved his theory, there were those who believed that they were attuned to them. On the other hand, it was quite plain that they were inaudible to the general run of men. Aristotle believed this was because familiarity from birth had inured them to it, in much the same way that a coppersmith became inured to the din about him. However, another explanation, and presumably one which accounted for Pythagoras's ability to hear them, was that they were audible only to the purest souls.

Under analysis, it becomes plain that the constituents of Pythagorean philosophy came from many different sources, in just the same way that the Cosmic Egg of the Orphics and the Serpent that issued from it had echoes not only in Phoenician and Mesopotamian myths, but also in those of the Old European civilization, whose beginnings predate even Sumer by perhaps as much as five thousand years.

It may be that, for us, the most striking thing about many of Pythagoras's prepositions is their falsity, even their naivety. None the less, accepting that they were perfectly consistent with the existing state of knowledge, what remains as a tribute to the qualities of his mind is how he united so much disparate knowledge into a coherent whole, one that was in many ways centuries before its time and that was to have so deep and telling an influence upon the generations of thinkers to follow.

9. The Roots of Pythagoreanism

In those passages in which I examined the details of Pythagoras's life I tried to indicate probable sources of some of his ideas. However, this procedure fails to set them in an overall context. It is certain that Pythagoras did not embark on his travels in the spirit in which an eighteenth-century English nobleman might pack his son off on the Grand Tour, in the vague belief that it would somehow improve his mind. He manifestly travelled with a definite object in view. He believed himself to have a mission and wished to fit himself to fulfil it; he wanted knowledge of a particular kind. We have seen that he was regarded as a magus or, as he was called in his own times, a *daimon*, so we can justifiably begin by supposing his travels were directed towards the acquisition of esoteric knowledge.

Such is the view of the Elder Pliny in *The Natural History*, for he writes:

> I have noticed that in ancient times, and indeed almost always, one finds men seeking in this science [he is referring to magic] the climax of literary glory – at least Pythagoras, Empedocles, Democritus and Plato crossed the seas, exiles, in truth, rather than travellers, to instruct themselves in this. Returning to their native lands, they vaunted the claims of magic and maintained its secret doctrine.

Many of the reported incidents in Pythagoras's life, as they have come down to us, especially his supposed miracle-working, have reminded some authorities, notably F. R. Dodds (*The Greeks and the Irrational*) of shamanism so strongly they have been led to posit a category of 'Greek shamans', of which Pythagoras was an example. In some ways, one is bound to agree, especially when one looks at shamanism closely.

Shamanism

Shamanism is more easily defined in terms of what it is not than of what it actually is. It is not a religion, for instance, nor are shamans priests. The mark of a religion is homogeneity of dogma and morality. It is part of the basic dogma of Christianity and Judaism that God is both creator and absolute master of the universe. Hence, his injunctions are to be obeyed in all circumstances. The needs of the individual, like those of the social group, are most reliably met by this unquestioning obedience and those who fail in it will be punished. The role of the priest is that of an interpreter in an unchanging system of beliefs. He is, at the same time, responsible for carrying out those communal liturgical functions of prayer and sacrifice by which belief is reinforced.

The shaman, though he may lay down the rituals to be carried out at the critical points of the year – the sowing, the harvest, the driving of the cattle to their summer pastures – is primarily concerned with the specific instance. If a ewe aborts, religion is likely to see this as a divine punishment and exhort greater, more unswerving obedience; the shaman seeks for other explanations through consultation with his familiar spirits. The most likely explanation is that the flocks have been afflicted by the malignity of some rival tribe. He will respond to this with his own counter-spell.

Some writers, like I. M. Lewis (*Ecstatic Religion*), have therefore described the shaman as one 'who has mastered the spirits and can at will introduce them into his own body'. But it is equally true that he can make contact with the spirits by leaving his body in cataleptic trance and visiting them in their Other World homes. Mircea Eliade, somewhat restrictively, defines the shaman solely in terms of this spirit-journey. As we have seen, it was one which Orpheus, like Aristeas and

Hermotimus of Klazomenai (all of whom Dodds numbers among his 'Greek shamans'), were also capable of making.

However, in societies where the shaman still flourishes he plays more than the single role of spirit mediator, central though it may be. His other functions include those of spell-caster, prophet and interpreter of portents. In many cases, he is credited with the ability to change his shape or to make himself invisible. He is also his tribe's healer, lawgiver, often its scribe and accountant, as well as mythologue and the singer of its epics.

This makes him a musician, an obvious parallel with Pythagoras, and one is reminded that early observers of the Celts, like Posidonius (*c.*131–151 BC), divided their religious leadership into Druids, Vates (or diviners) and Bards, though it is generally accepted that the three must at one time have been fused. Music was, accordingly, a part of shamanism and, indeed, in many cases the shaman induced trance through it, his drum being an essential item of equipment.

Intimacy with animal creation, which Pythagoras is reputed to have possessed, is another shamanistic trait, and the eagle has always been regarded as a much favoured creature. In some instances the god or spirit the shaman is seeking to invoke will take on its form, in others the shaman himself assumes it, but most often it is simply his familiar.

Also common to shamanistic systems is the concept of the Cosmic centre, of which an example is the World Tree, Yggdrasil, in Norse mythology. The centre is a theme that recurs in Celtic lore and is present in at least two existing place-names, Meath in the Irish Republic and Milan (originally Mediolanum) in northern Italy. Delphi, too, was a centre, being the *Omphalos* or navel of the world. Aristotle, who reproaches Pythagoras for his preoccupation with centres, since, as he says, geometrical centres are not necessarily particularly significant, misunderstands what is here meant. The shaman's centre is not a geometrical one at all. It was a place where the universal forces, those of earth, sky and underworld, are at their most potent and where men could make contact with them. This sets the Pythagorean doctrine in a totally different context.

The similarities between shamanism and Pythagoreanism

become even sharper when one looks at the training of recruits to the former, a subject on which we are now very well informed thanks to the first-hand studies of ethnologists and comparative religionists. Shamanism is a vocation *par excellence* in that he who seeks to pursue it believes himself called, sometimes by an inner sense of mission, sometimes by the spirits themselves who haunt his dreams or frustrate him in all undertakings.

Once he surrenders to them his novitiate comprises two elements which Eliade characterizes as the 'ecstatic' and the 'traditional'. The ecstatic includes a period of contemplation in some solitary place far from human habitation, recalling Pythagoras's experience in the Idaean caves of Crete; the traditional instruction is that instruction he receives at the hands of those already shamans who recognize him as one of themselves. It is they who will pass on to him, in the deepest secrecy and always by word of mouth, the mythology and lore of the calling. In this we have an analogy with the famous secrecy of the Pythagoreans and their insistence on the oral transmission of teachings. Originally the doctrines of Brahminism must also have been transmitted in this way, for much of it is in rhymes intended for easy memorizing, and that it was a characteristic of Druidism we know from Caesar's *The Conquest of Gaul*. Even Plato is said to have regarded oral teaching as superior to written.

Commenting on Dodds, J. A. Philip (*Pythagoras and Early Pythagoreanism*) says that shamans were not known among the Indo-Europeans. This is incorrect. Apart from the shamanistic traces to be found in Druidism, Brahminism and Magianism, the Scythian Enarees also bear the marks of such an ancestry.

In any case, the original homelands of the Indo-Europeans, in an area of the central Russian plain bounded by the Urals, the Caucasus and River Dnieper, were in close proximity to places where shamans have thrived throughout human history. But they must once have practised among the Greeks, too, for Greek mythology, like that of every other human society, is replete with those stories in which fundamental knowledge is revealed to mankind by some well-disposed deity, often in the teeth of opposition from his co-immortals. A typical example is the myth of Prometheus, the bringer of fire, but similar ones tell how man was taught to work metals or even how to ferment alcohol. The only feasible interpretation of these myths is that they represent the retelling, in symbolized form, of the shaman's trance-consultations with the inhabitants of the Other World, and Eliade is certainly right in calling Prometheus, like Apollo, a shamanistic god.

None the less, by the era of Pythagoras, the shaman, who is usually associated with a particular phase of social development, had long since disappeared from Greek life, leaving only his thumbprint on mythology. Dodds answers the difficulty this raises by suggesting that his 'Greek shamans' acquired their ideas from outside. His hypothesis is that the Scythians and the Getae were influenced by the shamanism of neighbouring, non-Indo-European peoples and that they, in their turn, influenced the Greek settlers on the shores of the Black Sea. The result was a sort of Hellenized shamanism centring round the worship of the Hyperborean Apollo.

In rejecting Dodds's theory of the 'Greek shamans', Philip points to the exalted position occupied by the shaman in his society. He is always close to the ruler; in some instances he actually occupies the position himself. Even where his role had undergone modification, as in Indian Brahminism or Celtic Druidism, he was still a highly privileged adviser. We are told, for instance, that Conchobhar, King of Ulster, spoke only after his three Druids had spoken. Pythagoras may have been deeply involved in the affairs of Croton, but there is little evidence that he was the city's shaman. Nor is there anywhere reference to his emulating such practices as those of MacRoth, the great Druid of King Ailill, who went into a trance and, in his invisible spirit form, went out to spy on the king's enemies; rather, the influence of the Pythagoreans was due to their moral character.

This suggests that while the Pythagoreans may have indulged in practices that had similarities with shamanism, they were themselves neither shamans nor the successors of shamans. However, since Pythagoreanism shows unmistakable shamanistic traits, they must have gathered them somewhere. I shall advance a somewhat different line of transmission from Dodds's, one which though more circuitous is, I believe, inherently more probable.

Pythagoreanism and Shamanism

Shamanism is usually to be found in its purest form among peoples practising nomadic pastoralism, such as the reindeer-herding Lapps of northern Europe. It also exists among the nomads of Siberia and Central Asia, from whom the word 'shaman' (= one who sees) has come into the language, as well as the American Indians, who are actually believed to have originated in Siberia, crossing the Bering Straits about 20,000 BC. It was Amerindian shamanism that was discovered by European settlers in North America in the 1870s and adopted as 'Spiritualism'.

In earlier times, shamanism was infinitely wider spread and would certainly have existed among peoples whose lands bordered Greece. These included the Thracians, whose *kapnobatai* induced trance states by inhaling the fumes of cannabis. There is every likelihood that Orpheus was himself a Thracian.

In many cases shamanism seems to survive the shift from nomadic to sedentary agriculture, though it undergoes some modification. The Celts, the Indians and the Persians were all at this stage, and Druidism, Brahminism and Magianism bear the marks of such modified shamanism.

Survival only began to be truly threatened with the emergence of the city-state. As Jacques Soustelle shows in *Les Quatres Soleils*, there is no smooth, evolutionary progression from village to city. The latter is an entirely different social phenomenon, one requiring a high degree of internal organization of a kind entirely absent in the village.

Wherever they went, the city-builders were invaders planting themselves precariously amid potentially and sometimes actively hostile populations. It was necessary not only for the newcomers to defend themselves by erecting defensive perimeters, but to achieve self-sufficiency. One manifestation of this was that the 'sacred grove' – the place in which they had formerly gathered for religious observances – had to be re-sited within the safety of the city's purlieus. It became the temple, its former character revealed in the pillars that were the rendering in architectural terms of the trees of the sacred grove.

The change which had taken place required a centralized,

omnipotent authority, one able to impose the necessary discipline to sustain it. This could only be made acceptable if divine sanction could be claimed for its rulers. They took over the role of mediators with the supernatural forces, ritualizing practice and making belief coincide with the interests and needs of the city-state. Such a secularizing process can, of course, be seen at work in the establishment and evolution of the Greek colonies and there is an instructive microcosm of it in the history of the Delphic Oracle. Originally appropriated by the shamanistic Apollo, it became increasingly an instrument of policy. In its latter days, there was scarcely more than a pretence that its utterances came from the inspired Pythia. It was the interpreter-priests who were responsible for them, consciously and deliberately producing 'prophecies' that fulfilled political needs.

In a number of cases the displacement of the shamans caused by the establishment of city-states extended as far as total banishment. This happened with the Hittites, for instance, among whom they survived only as 'wise men' (or, in many cases, 'wise women') consulted in secret as the witches were consulted in Europe later. This also seems to have happened with the Greeks for, apart from the mythological traces just discussed, there is little that is remotely shamanistic about the religion of Hesiod and Homer.

But in other cases the new rulers were prudent enough to realize that the shamans possessed useful knowledge. In such instances, instead of extirpation, they became, as it were, domesticated. While the prerogative of mediation with the high gods reposed solely with the king, the former shamans served him as astronomers royal, court physicians, advisers on the propitious moment to undertake some new enterprise.

Such a state of affairs came about in the Mesopotamian city-states. The first of these we know of is Sumer (though our picture of their evolution is likely to be altered as we understand the Old European cultures more fully). The ziggurats, so typical of Mesopotamian religion and of which the Tower of Babel is the most famous example, were undoubtedly intended to be centres, the man-made simulacra of some true centre recalled in myth or left behind in migrations.

In the Book of Daniel, which is the description of the prophet's exile with his companions in Babylon, the writer speaks of magicians, exorcists, sorcerers and Chaldeans or, sometimes, simply of 'wise men', who served the king. Whatever they were called, they were very different from the priesthoods familiar to the Greeks, and in Babylon, too, there was a totally separate body of priests responsible for temple worship. The fact that Daniel's 'wise men' were called in to interpret the royal dream indicates that the shamanistic practice of oneiromancy was known to them.

The Biblical account of them implies that they were more or less a group of impostors sponging on their royal master. This is the misrepresentation of a propagandist, for the repository of knowledge they possessed is one that has proved of fundamental importance to the human race, encompassing astronomy and highly developed mathematics. From Mesopotamia comes sexagesimal and decimal reckoning, the division of the circle into 360 degrees of arc, the extraction of square and cube roots, the formulae for calculating the circumference and area of the circle. In its schools the young were taught the Theorem of Pythagoras. The Biblical 'wise men' also invented phonetic writing and designed the spoked wheel that made possible lighter and speedier transport. They were, in fact, the world's first scientists.

Did they develop all these things after they had established themselves in their new homes in the Fertile Crescent, or did they bring the knowledge with them? There is reason for supposing – and the case is most plausibly made out by Geoffrey Ashe – that the latter is the case, and that they were convinced they had acquired it from contacts with a true and original centre which lay far to the north.

There is no space here to rehearse Geoffrey Ashe's arguments – they are, in any case, fully deployed in *The Ancient Wisdom* – but his main clue is the prevalence of the heptad, the Sacred Seven. This, as Apuleius (*c.*AD 155) tells us, was a significant number to the Pythagoreans, associated with 'things divine'. Ashe's trail leads, via all the myriad sevens from the seven-day week (another Sumerian invention), the seven storeys of the ziggurats, which symbolized the Seven Heavens, the seven notes of the musical scale so important to Pythagoreans, the seven colours of the spectrum, the Seven Deadly Sins and the Seven Cardinal Virtues, to the region dominated by the seven stars of the Great Bear, that very region in which the Greeks located the Land of the Hyperboreans and of Apollo.

It is a place that is still steeped in magic and where are located the legendary gold-bearing mountains of the Altai range. Within its boundaries lies Tibet, whose Bön magicians so impressed the eighth-century Buddhist missionaries that they sought initiation, and Bön-po practices, which included trance and spirit-flight, were absorbed into Tibetan lamaism. It is almost superfluous to recall that it is an area where there was an implicit belief in the transmigration of the soul long before it became part of Buddhist teaching.

On the high plateau of western Tibet stands Mount Kailas, which has been identified as Mount Meru or Sumeru, the golden mountain of the Hindus, the centre of the universe and the axis on which the world turns. It is the home of the gods, and among those who visited it were seven sages of such wisdom that they were regarded as semi-divine, in other words, as daimones. Hinduism equates them with the seven stars of the Great Bear – the constellation linked with the Hyperborean Apollo. This makes Sumeru very similar to the world mountain of Persian myth inhabited by seven gods.

The wide diffusion of ideas bearing the marks of an origin in the Altaic Zone has led some writers to postulate an ancient race of super-shamans, masters not only of magic, but also of astronomy and mathematics who came from there. Such a concept would give substance to stories passed on to the observers of contemporary shamans, who have told them of their distant ancestors beside whom they themselves were as mere shadows.

If at least part of the knowledge of the super-shamans was transmitted radially from their Altaic homelands in all directions, it would account for widely spread similarities of belief. Those between Pythagoreanism and the three eastern religions, Hinduism, Buddhism and Taoism, probably explain why some classical authors jumped to the conclusion that the travels of Pythagoras must have included India and, possibly, China.

Gautama Buddha and Lao Tzu, the semi-legendary founder of Taoism, were proselytizing at about the time of Pythagoras. Among the numerous points of coincidence in all three is the advocacy of a life of austerity and contemplation, whose object was union with what was called *Dharma* in Hinduism and Buddhism and *Tao* in China; both concepts possess many of the characteristics of Cosmos. Taoism and Buddhism also taught that everything in existence consisted of the intermixture of basic elements: where for the Pythagoreans these were four (earth, air, fire and water), the eastern religions taught there were five, though, of course, the Pythagoreans also had a fifth element in the form of the Divine Breath. (It is interesting, however, that the national flag of South Korea, a land where shamans flourished – and are still to be found – shows the four elements, earth, air, fire and water, at each of its corners.)

In addition, Tao had a list of antimonies that included the Pythagoreans' odd and even, odd being *yang* or masculine and even, *yin* or feminine. The others included the light-darkness of the Pythagoreans and activity-passivity, which corresponds with their moving-at-rest. The existence of another such list in Persian religion was, of course, one of the factors that led to assumption of the impossible – that Pythagoras had studied at the feet of Zoroaster.

Among those who appear to have imbibed the wisdom of the super-shamans were the founders of the Sumerian city-states. The racial origins of the Sumerians are unknown and may never be conclusively established, but from certain linguistic clues it has been tentatively suggested that they may have been of Mongoloid stock, which would locate their place of origin within the Altaic Zone. The esteem in which the knowledge of the Sumerians was held is indicated by the fact that not only did their conquerors, the Akkadians and the Assyrians, learn from them, but their language continued as a lingua franca of scholarship down to Babylonic times. It was contacts between the Babylonians and the Persian Medes that brought many of these ideas into Magianism; and it was their easterly neighbours, whose civilization was typified in their magnificent buildings, that the Greeks so envied and on which they so sedulously modelled themselves.

However, unlike the Greeks, who had shed their shamanistic tradition, with the Sumerians, Babylonians and Persians it remained very much alive among their 'wise men'; so when the Greeks began asking the obvious question – Where did they learn their wisdom? – the answer would have been that it came from contacts with that far northerly people and from men who were not only the fount of all knowledge but who had direct access to it because they dwelt near the Great Cosmic Centre, the real home of the gods. The Greeks named them 'the Hyperboreans', the People from Beyond the North Wind.

But with the legends there also went the cult of a god possibly identical with the one worshipped by the Mesopotamians as Shamash, lord of the sun, and, in one of his myths, the divine shepherd. He was also the inspirer of oracles, in this way providing not only glimpses into the future, but also handing down divine law to men.

The reasons for Pythagoras's travels and what he hoped to learn from them is now apparent. Aristeas made his fruitless journey in search of the Hyperboreans: his successor preferred to go to those who were thought to have been the direct inheritors of Hyperborean wisdom. It was they who provided him with his traditional lore, as the older shamans provided it for the newly initiated novices.

What he learnt from them he synthesized with elements of Orphism and the cult of the Idaean Zeus of Crete – both already containing elements from Mesopotamian religion – to forge his own original and unique system.

PART THREE: AFTER PYTHAGORAS

10. Dispersal and Dissemination

There was another rebellion in Croton some fifty years after the death of Pythagoras, that is to say in about 450 BC. By this time there must have been Pythagorean groups throughout the cities of Greece-in-Italy, for we are told that the revolt spread to them and that many were slaughtered and meeting houses and private homes were destroyed. Among them was that of Milo, the champion wrestler and successful commander in the war with the Sybarites.

This second catastrophe drove most of the surviving disciples from Magna Grecia, though a remnant seems to have stayed, re-forming in Rhegium.

By bringing about their dispersal, this, like other persecutions, had precisely the opposite effect from that intended by its perpetrators. Instead of erasing Pythagoreanism, it led to its wider dissemination. The reputation of its founder was such that his refugee-followers were welcomed wherever they went and new centres were established at Phlius in the Peloponnese, where they had contact with Socrates, and at Thebes on the Greek mainland. Here they were led by **Lysis,** teacher of Epaminondas, the commander of the Theban forces who defeated the Spartans at the Battle of Leuctra and later tutor to Philip of Macedon.

In choosing Thebes, the Pythagoreans must have been prompted by the thought that it was likely to prove a congenial environment. Not only had it been the centre of a bull-cult with many affinities to that of Dionysus subsumed into Orphism, but it also had a legendary founder, Amphion, son of Zeus by the nymph Antiope and another magic-musician like Orpheus and Pythagoras himself. Such was his skill that, at the bidding of his lyre, the very stones of which the walls of the city were built had leapt from the earth to take up their appointed places.

The Theban centre acquired a reputation that drew to it many of those Pythagoreans who had initially gone elsewhere. Among them was **Philolaus,** one of the principal interpreters of the master through whom, according to Diogenes Laertius, his teachings first began to be known to the outside world. Cebes and Simmias, the two Pythagoreans mentioned by Plato as being present at the death of Socrates, were said to have been his students. He does not, however, appear to have stayed permanently in Thebes but, when the fury of the mob had abated, returned to Italy, where his pupils may have included Archytas of Tarentum.

Archytas (400–500 BC), one of the most gifted of the successors of Pythagoras, has been called the founder of mechanical mathematics. He solved the problem of doubling the cube and applied the conclusions to the theory of music. In this way he did for Greek enharmonics what had earlier been done for the chromatic and diatonic scales by describing the mathematical ratios underlying them. It is also likely that Euclid borrowed from him for Book VII of *The Elements* and he was reputed to have carved a pigeon from wood that could actually fly – a feat others later tried to repeat. Typically, he combined all this with an active public life, serving for seven years as his city's commander-in-chief, though surprisingly for a Pythagorean he was a democrat. A personal friend of Plato's and thought by some to have been the author of parts of *The Republic*, he helped and counselled him during some of the most critical phases of his life.

After the move to mainland Greece, contacts between the separated groups became increasingly tenuous and in some cases ceased to exist. It has been suggested that for this reason, as age began to overtake the first generation of Pythagoreans, some may have felt that the need to preserve the teachings overrode the injunction to transmit them only by word of mouth.

In the greatest secrecy, they committed all they could remember to writing and before their deaths entrusted these invaluable documents to relatives or friends. Whether such action was taken we do not know, but no fragment of the memoirs has ever been found.

Diogenes Laertius is probably right in his assertion that the process of exposition began with Philolaus. It is, none the less, plain that he revealed only what he thought should be publicly known and that this was only a small part of the whole. In any case, caution is needed in assessing those statements alleged to have come from him. Not only is one relying on the memory of a single individual who may even have misunderstood the original teaching, but the personality of the writer, if it did not distort, would inevitably colour his interpretation.

Besides, men like Philolaus and Archytas viewed the doctrine dynamically, less as sacred and immutable utterance, than as knowledge to be expanded, developed and modified. The Greeks were often careless about attribution and the belief that it would add conviction to ascribe their ideas to a more august source could lead to Pythagoras becoming the originator of what had never in fact entered his mind.

This same process repeated among all the separated Pythagorean groups helped to bring about those confusions and often flat contradictions that have bedevilled us ever since and are now unlikely ever to be resolved.

Some of the problems arising in this way have been discussed earlier. A typical one is that of the hypothesis of the counter-earth and the central fire. Did Pythagoras actually teach that these were two separate and distinct entities, invisible to humanity because their motions corresponded exactly with those of the earth? Or was he the true originator of heliocentric astronomy, so that the counter-earth was a synonym for the moon, and the central fire the molten core of the earth? The second view is associated particularly with Philolaus, so was he faithfully recapitulating what he had learnt from his master or was he offering his own interpretation? And if the second, did he do so deliberately or had he misunderstood? Were there, as Guthrie appears to believe, two theories – the Philolaic, heliocentric, and the more commonly accepted geocentric one?

Perhaps, however, we should concern ourselves less with the niceties of Pythagorean belief and consider instead the ways in which, taken as a whole, it affected human thought. The supreme virtue of most new theories is in the way they illuminate particular kinds of phenomena rather than in the minutiae of the explanations they themselves offer. Wholly satisfactory explanations will be worked out only gradually and over a long period. Newton first proposed a law of gravity, yet while the existence of this force is generally accepted, no one today sees it in the terms in which he first expounded it.

Though Freud's doctrine of the Unconscious Mind has provided an important insight into human psychology, few would still describe its content or functions in precisely Freudian terms. History may well agree that Karl Marx's contribution to human understanding lies less in the detailed scenarios of *Das Kapital* than in the links he showed to exist between societies and their economies.

From the new centres, Pythagoreanism began to enter the mainstream of Greek philosophical thought – for example, through the contacts with **Socrates** (469–399 BC). How far Socrates's own ideas were shaped by them it is difficult to gauge with accuracy as our only sources are Xenophon and Plato in the *Dialogues,* and the second is suspected, though perhaps without reason, of using Socrates as a mouthpiece for his own theories. For all this, in one aspect, the minds of Socrates and of Pythagoras did resemble each other: both believed that the business of life was the tending of the soul. In these circumstances, it is hardly conceivable that Socrates would not have wanted to know what his predecessor had to say on the subject. The two men were of a profoundly mystical turn. Socrates was given to hearing voices and, according to Plato, fell into involuntary trances or 'rapts'.

There are other indications that Pythagoreanism had left its mark on the Athenian sage. He believed in the soul's immortality and its transmigration through various existences. He was fascinated by the Delphic Oracle and its god and adopted the maxim inscribed on the temple walls, 'Know thyself', as a principle of general validity. He lived a life of severe austerity and frequently of poverty.

In the case of **Plato** (*c.*427–348 BC), the evidence of Pythagorean mediation is clearer and one cannot but agree with Aristotle that it was Pythagoras who created the soil and atmosphere for him.

One of the implications of the doctrine of transmigration is explored in the *Meno*, where Plato presents the theory that knowledge is really recollection – that is to say, recollection carried over from one incarnation to the next back to some primordial time when it was first gained. This is exemplified by the instance of the young pupil who, though he has never studied the subject, can be brought to realize certain truths of mathematics because they already exist within him and he needs only prompting to recapitulate them.

But it is in *The Republic* that Pythagorean resonances are strongest. The guardians, the philosopher-kings of Plato's Utopian state, so strongly resemble, if not shamans, at least mages that some have suggested that he modelled them on legends of the Hyperborean 'super-shamans'. Their education is to include plane and solid geometry, astronomy and harmonics – all disciplines studied by the students of Pythagoras. The most important of all legislative acts, that of deciding religious practice, will be entrusted to Apollo, the expositor of 'all things to all men from his seat at the navel of the earth'.

While, in detail, Platonic and Pythagorean ideas are considerably at variance, they have a similarity in their overall cast. **Aristotle** (384–322 BC), who was Plato's pupil, declared that the doctrine of Forms did not much differ from the Pythagorean numerical concept. Plato denies that the basis of number was the Limited and Unlimited, though he speaks of the One, which incorporates the notions of limit, form and order as opposed to the Dyad, which is vague, limitless, potentially chaotic.

With Aristotle, a fundamental change comes over philosophy. He rejects the belief that the soul is 'punished' by imprisonment in the body and its corollary of repugnance for the physical as taught by Socrates, Plato and before them by Pythagoras. Instead, the physical, including the body, is seen as part of a benevolent creation and hence as a cause for celebration. At the same time, philosophy now chooses as its path that of a rational progression by logical steps from that which is apprehended by the senses. The intuitive, the revealed (and so unverifiable) is discarded and with it goes the notion of the liberation of the body from its 'prison' as represented by the shamanistic spirit-flight.

After Plato

Plato's immediate and practical contribution to the furtherance of philosophical inquiry was the foundation of his own school in the gymnasium at Academus, outside Athens. The Platonic academy continued after his death and was still flourishing at the time that Athens fell beneath the heel of Rome, when Cicero attended lectures there, though at the time Scepticism was the obtaining philosophy.

By the first century AD, when this was happening, Pythagoreanism was also undergoing a resurgence under the impetus of the mystical **Apollonius of Tyana** (b.*c.*4 BC), who claimed to be the reincarnation of Pythagoras and who wrote his biography.

His own was written by **Philostratus** at the instigation of the Empress Julia Domna, mother of Emperor Caracalla (AD 188–217), who was anxious to hold back the tide of Christianity. Like the late memorializers of Pythagoras, Philostratus gave himself the freedom to invent if he felt it would help to exhibit Apollonius as a pagan Messiah. There is no doubt, however, that he preached a regime of frugality, purity and occult wisdom and, especially, of emulation of the divine that was very much in the Pythagorean tradition. Another Neopythagorean **Nicomachus of Gerasa** (*c.*AD 100), whose *Introduction to Arithmetic*, the first book to use Arabic numbers, was for a thousand years a standard textbook, wrote another on the subject of number-mysticism.

By the late second century AD, Pythagorean ideas were being explored in Platonism. Anti-Aristotelianism became more and more widespread and the tendency towards speculative theology and occult practices, including trance induction, stronger. With the similarities between them, it was only to be expected that the two would merge, particularly as in many quarters it was felt that pagan philosophy needed to form a united front against the inroads of Christianity. The amalgam was **Neoplatonism,** developed by **Plotinus** (b.*c.*AD 205) in the third century, and it is through it that the Pythagorean line has to be traced hereafter.

The new phenomenon was not entirely to be explained in terms of the fusion of Neopythagoreanism with Platonism. Orthodox Christianity was by no means the only religious movement gaining ground at the time. Among the pagan religions, there was Mithraism, basically the worship of the Zoroastrian god of justice and counterpart of the Hindu Mitra, though by these late times myth and theology had taken on a markedly Platonic hue, with Pythagorean and Orphic elements being intermingled. It was one of the many factors that helped to shape what ultimately became a Christian heresy: **Gnosticism.**

The roots of Gnosticism lay in Zoroastrian dualism as well as in Mesopotamian and Egyptian thought. Since Pythagoras and, through him, Plato had drawn from the same well, it was inevitable that there should be correspondences between Gnostic and Platonic ideas. Their respective cosmologies both taught that the Cosmos was made up of a succession of concentric spheres descending hierarchically so that the last ones were the universe and earth, perceptible to the physical senses. In Gnosticism, as in early Platonism, the spirit once more becomes the captive longing for escape and the notions of trance and visionary flight, as means of gaining *gnosis* or knowledge, reappear.

Unlike in the sixth century BC, when it was only an intellectual élite that was conscious of the inadequacies of religion and turned to the Mysteries and to philosophies like that of Pythagoras as an alternative, now it was every class that had lost its faith and wanted a new one. To ordinary men and women, unequipped to choose between competing creeds, it can only have been a time of desperate confusion, when all they knew was that the old certainties were certainties no longer. Whenever some new pedlar of marvels appeared, they must have turned to him gratefully. And of these there was, as always in such times, no shortage. Some were, no doubt, genuine in the belief that they were inspired; others were unscrupulous charlatans; yet others were those who, on the principle of restoring the old beliefs and stabilities, did not scruple to use any means to do so.

Two such were Porphyry and Iamblichus. In **Porphyry** (AD 233–*c.*301), a pupil of Plotinus's, the esoteric aspects of Platonism were given strong emphasis while in those of his own pupil, **Iamblichus** (d.*c.*AD 330), Neoplatonism was expanded into a metaphysical system, a complete alternative to Christianity. Belief in a god who interested himself directly in the affairs of men was, of course, part of the cult of Apollo. Now it was shared by the other Immortals. The planets, metals, precious stones, animals, fish, herbs and other plants were placed under the protection of one deity or another, which is why Graeco-Roman god-names so often form part of the botanical nomenclature of our familiar garden flowers. At the same time, each was allotted his or her sphere of influence in the everyday life of mortals. This idea was by no means new. It was to be found in Mesopotamian religion and had probably existed in Greece, if only in implicit form. However, divine benevolence was hardly a characteristic of Greek religion in its Heroic Age. The gods of Homer are marked by capriciousness rather than fundamental goodwill towards men. The full development of the idea was obviously intended as an answer to the God of loving-kindness portrayed in Judaism and Christianity. This, it must be remembered, was the time when the struggle for souls was reaching its apogee with Julian the Apostate (emperor AD 361–3) assuming the purple and struggling to re-establish paganism.

Iamblichus, like Porphyry, produced an idealized life of Pythagoras that was intended to show him as being comparable with Christ. The fact that two leading Neoplatonists chose Pythagoras as the subject of major works shows how important an influence he was thought to exert.

The Egyptian victories of Alexander the Great (356–323 BC) and his foundation of Alexandria as a Greek city on the Nile brought about a diffusion of Platonism, as well as of other Greek philosophies, among the people of the large and well-educated Jewish community of that city. One of those who applied them to Judaism was **Philo of Alexandria** (*fl.* AD 39) and it is plain from Paul's address before the Areopagus that he was not unacquainted with Greek thought. It was from Alexandria, too, that it was destined to enter an Islamic tradition culminating in philosophers like **Avicenna** (Ibn Sina, 980–1037) and **Averroes** (Ibn Rushd, 1126–1198), who were later to influence western thinking.

11. Pythagoras and the Renaissance

The era of the pagan revival, that of Porphyry and Iamblichus, had seen the appearance of the *Chaldean Oracles,* purporting to be a compendium of Zoroastrian mystical teaching but actually a regurgitation of odds and ends of Greek religious philosophy. Though Porphyry treated them with some caution, Iamblichus gave every sign either of accepting them wholeheartedly or, at any rate, of appearing to do so for his own purpose.

In an age of such counterfeits, there was also another, the *Corpus Hermeticum,* a collection of writings supposedly inspired by Hermes Trismegistus (Hermes the Thrice Great). This time Pythagorean and Platonic philosophy had assumed an Egyptian mantle, the author claiming to be a priest of the Egyptian Thoth, identified with the Greek Hermes. Since the Greeks were supposed to have acquired their religion from Egypt, the remarkable correspondences between the Hermetic literature and their own philosophers did not cause much surprise and they were, therefore, accepted as genuine.

In spite of the term 'The Dark Ages' to designate the period from the fall of Rome in the fifth century AD to the coronation of Charlemagne in the eighth, and of the 'Renaissance' to signify the revival of classical learning, the discontinuity that this implies had not in fact occurred. Christian apologists had been employing the methods of Greek philosophy no less than their Moslem and Jewish counterparts, and St Augustine (354–430), the missionary dispatched to bring England under the sway of the Roman Church, was an eminent Christian Platonist, though the distinctions between it and Aristotelianism had, by this time, become considerably blurred.

The re-separation of the two strains owes much to **Nicholas de Cusa** (1401–64), a German priest, given his cardinal's hat in the 1440s. An outstanding mathematician as well as a philosopher and a theologian, he argued against Aristotle's doctrine of the incompatibility of contradictories – as, for example, between the straight line and circle. Such doctrines were, in his view, a bar to the understanding of God, who, because he was infinite, was able to reconcile all such opposites.

This he demonstrated by means of geometry. The larger the circle, the less the curvature of its circumference. Hence, were it possible to inscribe an infinite circle, the circumference would become a straight line. Aristotle was dethroned in favour of his predecessors, Plato and Socrates. The description of the learned man de Cusa gives in his *De docta ignorantia* (Of the Ignorance of the Learned), is one fully in accord with the Socratic view, for his learned man is one who recognizes his own ignorance.

One of Nicholas's most fervent admirers was **Marsilio Ficino** (1433–99), a Florentine scholar and magus. A Byzantine visitor to his city, Pletho, a fanatical pagan Platonist, persuaded Cosimo de'Medici, the rich chief magistrate, that he should have the works of the master translated. An obvious choice for the task was Ficino, but before he was properly embarked on it another Greek manuscript came into Cosimo's possession and the description of its contents, given him by the Macedonian monk who delivered it, set him in such a fever of excitement that he insisted that everything else be put aside while it was first translated.

It was the *Corpus Hermeticum* and, thanks to Cosimo's impatience, it was one of the first works of classical scholarship to be devoured throughout Europe. No one doubted its authenticity and that it dated back to a time at least contemporary with and quite possibly earlier than that of Moses. As it prophesied the collapse of pagan polytheism and its replacement by monotheism, as well as what could only be interpreted as the Christian revelation, its author was promptly elected to the *prisco theologi*, the blessed pagans.

Though there were Gnostic and Stoic, as well as Zoroastrian and Jewish, influences present in it, the *Corpus Hermeticum* was primarily Neoplatonic; it was thus very much to the taste of the period and was responsible for bringing the ideas of Pythagoras back into currency. For Ficino and his fellow-Florentine magus, **Pico della Mirandola** (1463–94), it was Pythagoras, through the mediation of his disciples, Philolaus, who had been the teacher of their 'Divine Plato'.

The various treatises of which the *Corpus* is made up cover such topics as astrology, magic, alchemy, philosophy as well as a theology largely Gnostic in character, the whole being couched in a portentous and turgid style which makes their reading an ordeal. Not only did they seem to cast an entirely new light on pagan thought, they also raised the hitherto proscribed practice of magic to respectability.

The *Corpus* prompted men to re-read the Greek philosophers, as well as giving them grounds for hoping that an entirely new theology could be forged, one that would reunite Christianity, so that even orthodox prelates like Nicholas de Cusa adopted Hermeticism. In England, Thomas More translated a biography of Pico della Mirandola which mentions his interest in the secret mysteries of the Hebrews, Chaldeans and Arabs. The last is almost certainly a reference to Islamic philosopher-scientists like Avicenna and Averroes, who were not only highly regarded but also believed to be magi. In the same passage, More also refers to the 'old, obscure philosophy of Pythagoras, Trismegistus and Orpheus'.

Across the length and breadth of Europe men began experimenting in magic and number mysticism *à la* Pythagoras. *Nous*, the intuitive faculty, had re-entered the human awareness and was to be actively cultivated.

In *Corpus Hermeticum II*, a personified *Nous* tells Hermes that, if he wishes to do so, he can command his soul to travel to India or to ascend to the stars and the furthermost reaches of the universe. This is plainly spirit-flight, the gnostic trance which Pythagoras was credited with practising, and which occurs in the legends of Hermotimus of Klazomenai and Aristeas of Proconnesus. If there is any doubt on this score, Pico settles it in his *Conclusiones Cabalisticae* when he speaks of a supreme trance in which the spirit is separated from the body.

How much was Pythagoreanism consciously at work in this? Obviously a great deal. Ficino experimented with solar magic and chanted Orphic hymns; Pico believed that in numbers lay the key to understanding the universe. The English magus, **John Dee** (1527–1608), astrologer to Mary Tudor and her successor, Elizabeth I, and regarded as one of the greatest minds in Europe, believed, like Pythagoras, that heat, cold, moisture and dryness constituted the true 'temperaments' of everything. He interested himself in musical magic, listing among those who had performed wonders through it Orpheus, Amphion, the founder of Thebes, the psalmist David and Pythagoras. At the same time he regarded Pythagorean number-mysticism as fundamental to his whole philosophy. For this reason, he separated mathematics into two branches: the practical – he wrote works for the guidance of those who needed mathematical knowledge in their daily work as well as the preface to the English translation of Euclid – and that of an esoteric kind which he called 'mathesis'.

He believed that through number it was possible to induce the gnostic-trance and in one passage virtually paraphrases *Nous* to Hermes, saying that through contemplation (i.e., of number), the mathematician can 'Mount above the Cloudes and sterres' in the process learning the secrets of nature, which he can 'frame to wonderful uses'. It is doubtful whether Dee actually tried experiments of this kind, but he employed a medium, Edward Kelley, probably a fake, who in trance was supposed to be able to contact angels to whom he put his employer's questions, the latter recording the entire colloquy.

Pythagorean motifs are also in evidence in Dee's *Monas Hieroglyphica,* the title page of which shows the 'London Seal of Hermes' with a circle surmounted by an arc above a cross. Everything, he explains, derives from the circle and the straight line, both of them generated by a moving point. Hence the beginning of all things is the point and the monad.

Another early Renaissance magus, **Heinrich Cornelius Agrippa** (1486–1535), regarded Pythagoras as one of the founders of his calling. In his *De occulta philosophia,* he endeavoured to explain the world in terms of Hebrew gematria and number-mysticism, which, he believed, operated on a super-celestial level. Everything in nature was governed by such characteristics as weight and measure, which could be expressed in terms of number. By mathematics it was possible to produce such great wonders as statues that moved and spoke – an allusion here not only to the moving, speaking statues of the Egyptians mentioned in the *Corpus*, but also to such amazing artefacts as the dove of Archytas. However, it has to be remembered that the mathematics of the time included mechanics and it was through applied mathematics that musical grottoes, singing fountains and speaking sculptures like those in the castles of Heidelberg described by Frances Yates in *The Rosicrucian Enlightenment* were operated.

Frances Yates's book also touches on the Pythagorean borrowings of the **Rosicrucian movement** at its beginnings in the seventeenth century and, in particular, the use of the so-called Pythagorean Y in its symbolism. The letter is used to represent the choice between two paths, the virtuous and the vicious, and has a distinctly Orphic ring about it, reminiscent of the instructions inscribed on the gold sheets found in Italy that tell the soul of the newly-deceased how to find the Afterworld of the Blessed.

Giordano Bruno (1548–1600), perhaps in many ways the most illustrious and influential of the Renaissance magi, repeatedly summoned Pythagoras in support of his theses. These included a belief in a heliocentric, infinite universe, a suggestion that appears to have emanated from Nicholas de Cusa. Thus, whether Pythagoras himself actually taught heliocentricity or not, he was responsible for directing the minds of men towards it and it was certainly from the consideration of Pythagorean and Philolaic speculations on the subject that Copernicus began to ponder seriously the thesis he was to expound in his devastating *De revolutionibus orbium caelestium* (On the revolution of the celestial spheres).

However, even the briefest review of the Pythagorean thought of the Renaissance cannot omit one of the greatest of those directly influenced by it. This was **Johann Kepler** (1571–1630), discoverer of the principles of planetary motion. Unlike many of his time, he did not take the Music of the Spheres literally, but believed that the heavenly bodies were governed by what might be called a 'harmonious interrelation', which was also to be found in arithmetic and geometry as in music.

* * * * *

Perhaps the Establishment, both of state and of Church, and as much in Protestant as Catholic countries, had become alarmed by the implications of Platonism and Pythagoreanism. In the last decade of the fifteenth century, thirty years after the death of the great Cardinal Nicholas de Cusa, and in a vastly changed atmosphere, Giordano Bruno was arrested on charges of heresy. The proceedings against him began under the auspices of the Venetian Inquisition and seemed likely to end in his acquittal. Then in January 1493, he was extradited to Rome to face its Inquisition. The trial lasted seven years, but on 8 February 1600 he was formally sentenced to death and, nine days later, burned alive at the misnamed Field of Flowers.,

His passing could be said also to mark the passing of the heyday of the Renaissance magus, in whose creed Pythagoreanism had figured so prominently. It was only fourteen years later than the penetrating Gallic mind of **Isaac Casaubon** (1559–1614) recognized that the *Corpus Hermeticum* was a post-Christian production. It was not prophesying miraculously; it was reporting what had already come to pass. Not everyone was convinced by his arguments and in his own adopted country, England, the magus and Rosicrucian **Robert Fludd** (1554–1637), who was in many ways the intellectual successor to John Dee, still called them in witness. Even **Isaac Newton** (1642–1727), born five years after Fludd's death, was influenced by them, having encountered the Hermetic tradition from his reading of the Cambridge Platonist, Henry More. The last of the great seventeenth-century philosophers to believe himself a true follower of Pythagoras was the German **Gottfried Wilhelm Leibniz** (1646–1716), a contemporary of Newton's.

12. Pythagoras and the Western Esoteric Tradition

In the last chapter we looked briefly at the influence of Pythagorean thought on those primarily Christian mages who began to emerge during the Renaissance. Like their Greek models, they claimed to have knowledge of an esoteric kind and, indeed, are often spoken of simply as 'the esoterics' on this account.

In very broad terms, esoteric knowledge can be defined as that restricted to those within a prescribed, exclusive, often secret body. Being secret it is the converse – though not necessarily, the opponent – of exoteric knowledge, that which is available to anyone who applies to the right books or to suitably qualified teachers. The seeker for esoteric knowledge must not only prove his academic credentials, as it were, but also those moral ones that fit him for discipleship, because, it is argued, the knowledge he hopes to receive is such as will impart enormous power, with the consequent risk of abuse by the unworthy.

A modern analogy, and one frequently drawn by esoterics themselves, is between a learner driver and one who wants to enter a learned profession. The only concern of the driving instructor is to impart to his pupil such skill and knowledge as will enable him to pass the driving test by helping him to become familiar with the operation of the car, with the intricacies of driving in all kinds of traffic and with the rules of the Highway Code. Whether the pupil is faithful to his wife or involved in embezzling his employers is no affair of the instructor's, though even a driving instructor would, presumably, hesitate to pass his knowledge on to one with a history of chronic alcoholism or mental instability.

In the case of entry to one of the learned professions, on the other hand, the applicant has to satisfy his putative instructors of his temperamental suitability for it. The various tests, interviews and interrogations, for example, that a potential medical student has to undergo are aimed very largely at discovering this and have their counterpart, esoterics would say, in the often exhaustive preliminaries and, in some cases, rituals to which applicants must submit.

However, the analogy is far from complete. Once he is accepted by a medical school, the new student will learn his vocation by way of books, lectures, demonstrations and the personal instruction of teachers. Not so the novice esoteric. Though these play their part in his studies, it is a subsidiary one and the role of teacher will be primarily that of helping him to cultivate in himself a refined intuitive faculty that leads, if he possesses the adequate innate gifts, to the ability to induce trance.

It is obviously no part of this work to follow the progression by which the attributes of the magus – in whom, it could be said, the development of intuitive faculties was combined with those activities we usually associate with philosophical speculation and of the natural scientist – fragmented, to the point at which the three divided and, to a very considerable extent, went their respective ways.

There is little doubt that in this division, the intuitive component, if not utterly abandoned and forgotten, fell into abeyance. In so far as it survived, it can be said to have been represented by two figures. One is the supposedly fourteenth-century religious sage Christian Rosenkreuz (= Rose Cross), the other the indisputably real William Blake (1757–1827). The latter's essentially revolutionary (not to say anarchistic) view of human society was always bound up with his mystical and visionary outlook, and it was this which drew him to study what were then called the Ancient Britons or, as we know them, the Celts. It also brought him into contact with the work of the Neoplatonist Thomas Taylor, to whom several references have already been made.

The principal written account of the foundation of Rosicrucianism – a specifically Christian manifestation – is contained in the *Fama Fraternitatis,* published in 1614 and usually attributed to V. V. Andreae, and which purports to describe the journeys of Rosenkreuz. He is said to have received the secret wisdom of the Egyptians, Syrians and Arabs, which he passed on to three German disciples. Their number was later increased to eight and they were dispatched to different countries to make converts. Like most similar movements, the Rosicrucians claim considerable antiquity, even numbering Plato, Jesus and Plotinus among their former members, though most scholars are unanimous in averring that there is no sign of its existence prior to the seventeenth century. It is now generally agreed that the story of their foundation is more or less of a fiction invented by Andreae and intended to be taken symbolically, as is indicated by the name of the founder.

Frances Yates, who has written a definitive study of the movement, describes the considerable following it attracted in the seventeenth century, including among it European royalty. She also points out the numerous Pythagorean traits to be found in Rosicrucianism, which may have descended from the *Corpus Hermeticum*.

The next and, for our own epoch, more significant revival had to wait until the middle of the nineteenth century and H. P. Blavatsky.

Helena Petrovna Hahn was born in 1831 in the Ukraine. In the 1840s she married an officer named Blavatsky, but appears to have left him after only a few months of marriage. Like Pythagoras (and Christian Rosenkreuz), she then embarked on a series of travels which, according to her own accounts, took her through most of the Orient, including Japan, India and Tibet, where she claimed to have received enlightenment.

In 1873 she was in New York. Here she met Henry Steel Olcott, a lawyer accorded the honorary rank of colonel on account of work for the US War and Navy Departments, but who nursed philosophical ambitions. With him she organized a group devoted to the study of occult phenomena and in the 1870s this became the nucleus of the Theosophical Society, initially with only sixteen members. In 1879, they jointly established the first Theosophist Temple at Adyar, near Madras. Among those who were drawn to it was the British Socialist and founder of the Indian independence movement, Annie Besant, who became presidence of the Theosophical Society from 1907 until her death at Adyar in 1933.

Madame Blavatsky's philosophy is expounded in *Isis Unveiled* and *The Secret Doctrine*, as well as through the Society's journal, *The Theosophist,* of which she was editor for many years.

The last phase of her life was devoted to the study of occult phenomena and in 1888 she established an Esoteric Section of the Theosophical Society. She died in London in 1891.

Both in her lifetime and subsequently, Madame Blavatsky has been the subject of much immoderate and frequently unfair criticism. Her books were said to have been plagiarized from works in Henry Olcott's library; as a spiritist medium, she was accused of fraud, while intellectually, she has been charged with lack of rigour, of inconsistency and of failure to support her claims with evidence.

Even with these criticisms accepted, however, she must still be regarded as a pioneer in two respects. She reintroduced to the Western consciousness an awareness of a dimension missing for over a century and which the reductionist, scientific determinism of the time seemed set fair entirely to obliterate. She also awakened an interest in Eastern religion, which has never since been entirely lost and which, to some extent, is now beginning to influence even Christian thought. Thus she can be credited with pioneering the line which led to such extraordinary people as Alexandra David-Neel, who brought to the West such astonishing descriptions of Tibetan mysticism.

Madame Blavatsky's adoption of the term 'theosophy', which means 'knowledge of God', to describe her movement is significant. Despite an outwardly religious, and in some cases specifically Christian, ethos, and for all that they demand of those who come to study their teachings a high moral charcter, esoteric systems could be said to place their emphasis on reaching the divine through the acquisition of knowledge rather than through belief and conduct.

The expression 'knowledge of God' also reminds one of Gnosticism, an association of the Theosophists would by no means have disclaimed, and it is of course in the tradition of Socrates, who taught that men and women erred only from knowing no better and that, once having apprehended ultimate truths, would, willy-nilly, follow them. In this way, knowledge could be said to affect conduct. It is, besides, proper to observe that the importance of belief and conduct is by no means ignored in most esoteric systems, which seek to bring about what are called 'the two unions': the occult one of merging the self with the universe, and the mystical one of mergence with the Divine by means of absolute devotion. These unions are inextricably interdependent.

The Theosophical Society is now, of course, only one of a large number of esoteric bodies representing a broad spectrum of often radically divergent opinion, and it is certainly true that, at any rate to the layman, the apparent inconsistencies to be found in Theosophy, as in the rest, makes it difficult to attempt any kind of summary of their teaching. One also has to contend with a secrecy which, in many ways, is like that of the Pythagoreans, while the teachings are themselves complex and, therefore, open to misinterpretation.

There is, none the less, a common core running through them: all distinguish their own type of knowledge from exoteric knowledge, the former being available solely through mystical experience.

As the first source of this knowledge most posit the existence of a class of quasi-divine masters (e.g., Madame Blavatsky's Tibetan mahatmas). According to some, these Masters are incarnate as human beings; to others they are discarnate and hence approachable only in trance. Their membership includes the Hindu Krishna, Jesus of Nazareth, the Buddha, Lao Tzu, Confucius and Muhammad, as well as Orpheus, Hermes, Euclid, and Pythagoras, the supposed founder of a Western esoteric tradition whose name is commemorated in the so-called 'Pythagorean Ray', that of Abstract Mind.

The Masters were the intellectual élite among an Ur-race of supermen, the men of Hesiod's Golden Age, who have now disappeared from the earth. One explanation of this is that they were destroyed when the continent of Atlantis was engulfed by the melting of the polar cap. Fortunately, the loss was not complete. Being warned prophetically of the cataclysm, a group of the Masters migrated, one sign of their passage being the standing stones they erected. These are to be found from North Africa up the western seaboard of Europe, across the British Isles and as far north as the Baltic – though, it must be noted, there are also a few examples to be found in the Far East, as on Kanghwa Island off the west coast of South Korea.

The Masters gradually withdrew from the mortal plane, though not before leaving the imprint of their teaching upon all the world's religions.

Plainly their wisdom was not of a merely physical kind; it encompassed what we call the 'paranormal', though to them and to the followers of all esoteric systems there is no separate category of the paranormal but total continuity between its phenomena and those of natural science. It is only by virtue of a later misconception, regarded by some as the product of Man's own fallen or, at any rate, primitively undiscerning nature that the two are now at odds.

At some time in an undefined future humanity's sensitivities will develop sufficient acuity for the error to be recognized and corrected. We shall then perceive the universe to be a unity, essentially spiritual and so quite different in nature from that which we apprehend with our unregenerate physical senses.

I am aware that in this attempt to restate esoteric belief I have been guilty of gross oversimplification and that its advocates will be able to find omissions and misrepresentations. For this I duly apologize, though I believe even this bald summary serves to make clear the parallels with Pythagoreanism.

There is, for instance, the secrecy and the creation of an élite of disciples whose members are required to prove their moral, as much as their intellectual qualities. There is the primacy of knowledge and, as a corollary, the conviction that this can in itself light the path to redemption. More significantly, there is the belief that the most desirable form of knowledge is attainable only through a species of mystical experience.

The semi-divine Masters bring to mind the *daimones* of Pythagoras, of which he was himself one, and the race of supermen from which they spring obviously suggest the Hyperboreans. On such a reading, Apollo, chief of the

Pythagorean deities, becomes less like a deity than another Master, a position close to the one Pythagoras himself might have adopted. Many of the esoteric systems declare that the Masters were taken as gods by the ignorant and superstitious.

The view of the universe as informed by spirit is also strikingly like the Pythagorean Cosmic one.

But do they derive from Pythagorean sources? Madame Blavatsky herself always said she took them from the eastern religions and there is no reason to doubt her. At the same time, the fact that similar ideas were to be found among the Greeks would obviously have suggested to her either an interconnection or that both were derived from one system. Indeed, her informants would no doubt have assured her this was the case.

We have previously examined the persistence of belief in a Sacred Centre whose inhabitants include seven, semi-divine Masters and which was probably current in some form in the time of Pythagoras. Before taking this either as collateral proof of the existence of the Greeks' Hyperboreans, one must not lose sight of the fact that in the enormous time which had elapsed there was ample opportunity for borrowing and re-borrowing and that, indeed, the Greeks actually conquered much of the Indian subcontinent.

It would certainly be extremely rash to conclude from this that we can assume Pythagorean doctrines to be similar in all respects to those which Madame Blavatsky found on her eastern travels.

Lastly, even if it could be established that such Pythagorean mediation as can be recognized in the beliefs of the latterday western esoterics has an incontrovertibly Greek provenance, it still seems more likely to have been derived, not from the original, but from his distant successors, the Neoplatonists, in whom, partly from the erosion of time and partly from other factors, including political ones, substantial alteration had taken place.

* * * * *

A question remaining to be asked is, what is the nature of the knowledge of which esoterics claim to be the possessors, and how far does it resemble that of the Pythagoreans? It is, predictably, impossible to answer. Sceptics who suggest that this is due to its non-existence are, naturally enough, not lacking. Esoterics themselves would say it was due solely to the secrecy in which their knowledge is and has always, of necessity, been shrouded.

It is true that a few fragmentary hints come to us via astrology or through the beliefs of those who interest themselves in matters like the supposed interconnections between such things as planets, minerals, colours, flora and fauna, themes developed in philosophies like those of Rudolf Steiner. To the outsider, while these interconnections may suggest the Pythagorean Cosmos, they are also too nebulous to allow for adequate comparison.

However, the esoteric might go on to add that much of his formerly arcane knowledge has gradually, thanks to the intercession of the Masters in human affairs, become known. As illustration, he could cite the theory of evolution, always part of his own doctrines, but only recently absorbed into the corpus of the scientific world view. He might add that writing and mathematics, formerly esoteric pursuits, are now entrusted to every child. As one writer puts it, the progress of humanity has largely been in terms of esoteric wisdom becoming exoteric, the repository of the first being thereby diminished.

There is a certain superficial plausibility in the argument, but it is only superficial. At some remote period in human history it is quite possible that mathematics was a science reserved for an élite. As we saw, as late as the sixteenth century a distinction was drawn between practical mathematics and *mathesis*, which, however, was largely in the nature of gematria and other forms of numerology. None the less, the cuneiform tablets make it plain that the Sumerians taught very advanced mathematics indeed to their children four millennia ago.

Secondly, not all esoteric knowledge has stood the test of time. There is no doubt that men like Fludd and Dee believed in the Harmony of the Spheres. It might be answered that they understood it, as Kepler did, purely in a symbolical sense. The fact is that this is a defence all too readily available and all too readily adopted in an awkward situation. Any thesis which is disproved can be explained as having only symbolical intention.

And what of esoterics' version of the Theory of Evolution? Since it is no longer secret, it would redound greatly to their credibility if they now produced documentary proof that their own concept of it was on all fours with the scientific one.

* * * * *

An aspect of Pythagoreanism meriting more than the scanty examination I must accord it is its influence on Christian theology and mysticism itself. This was very considerable and is perhaps not entirely unexpected, since Pythagoras, like Plato and Socrates, was numbered among the *prisci theologi*.

Robert Graves, in a footnote in *The White Goddess*, touches on the topic, though, alas, without development, contenting himself with citing the single instance of the eleventh century Bernard of Morlaix, born in Brittany of English parents. He was the author of devotional, largely ecstatic, works in one of which he pays specific tribute to Pythagoras.

Bernard was accused of pantheism, but as Graves points out, the charge was without foundation and in fact he went no further than to suggest that connections between, for example, certain natural manifestations – a view wholly consistent with the Pythagorean concept of Cosmos – could cast a revelatory light on the Christian mysteries.

There are, of course, those who attribute both the doctrine of the Trinity and the practice of speaking of God as 'the One' to Pythagorean influence, and in the second case they may be right. It is at least curious, if not more, that among the hymns in praise of the Holy Trinity in *Hymns Ancient and Modern*, two, 163 and 655, have strongly Orphic if not Pythagorean resonances. With its emphasis on the One and its equating of the Deity with the sun – mentioned as both rising and setting – 163 could well have been intended for addressing to Apollo. Hymn 655 is full of astronomical allusions and the theme of binding, while one of its rather lengthy verses seems to be an invocation against magic spells.

It is surely our own age that, more than any other, has written the epilogue to Pythagoras and the Pythagoreans. It is the age which takes for granted the truly astonishing fact that the complex chemical structure of an organic substance can be adequately described in a few capital letters and fewer numbers. It is the age when, in the wake of Einstein's *General Theory of Relativity,* physicists, without the least self-consciousness, can declare that their aim is to discover the equations that will account for the entire universe. Even Pythagoras himself might have blanched at such presumption!

Much of the drudgery of the task of authors like myself has been abolished by the word-processor, which is really just another application of the ubiquitous electronic-computer. As we type our words, it meticulously translates them into numbers, which are the computer's only language, then back into the letters that flash across the monitor screen; ultimately, through the medium of instructions, also converted into numbers, it types out what has been written at a speed greater than that of the most accomplished professional typist.

Even the sonorities of the symphony orchestra, unimaginably more complex than those of the *kithara* and *aulos* of Pythagoras's time, are now capable of being recorded 'digitally', to be reproduced with an accuracy far beyond the most sophisticated high-fidelity equipment of the past.

The age in which everything has truly become 'assimilated to number' is, surely, the one over which Pythagoras deserves to be the presiding daimon.

Select Bibliography

Ashe, Geoffrey, *The Ancient Wisdom* (London, 1977).
Bernal, J. D., *Science in History* (London, 1954).
Boyce, Mary, *The Zoroastrians* (London, 1979).
Bury, J. B., Cook, B. A., and Adcock, F. E., *The Cambridge Ancient History*, vol. iv, *The Persian Empire and the West* (Cambridge, 1969).
De Vogel, *Pythagoras and the Early Pythagoreans* (New York, 1965).
Dickinson, G. Lowes, *Plato and His Dialogues* (Harmondsworth, 1931).
Diels, Herman, and Kranz, Walther, *Die Fragmente Vorsokratiker* (Berlin, 1951).
Diogenes (Laertius), *La Vie de Pythagore* (Brussels, 1922).
Eliade, Mircea, *Shamanism: The Archaic Technique of Ecstasy* (Princetown University Press, 1972).
French, Peter, *John Dee* (London, 1972).
Ghyka, Matila, *Geometrical Composition and Design* (London, 1952).
Gimbutas, Marija, *The Gods and Goddesses of Old Europe* (London, 1974).
Gorman, Peter, *Pythagoras – A Life* (London, 1979).
Graves, Robert, *The White Goddess* (London, 1977).
Gunn, Peter, *Southern Italy* (London, 1959).
Guthrie, W. K. C., *A History of Greek Philosophy*, vol. 1 (Oxford, 1962).
——, *Orpheus and Greek Religion* (London, 1935).
——, *The Greeks and their Gods* (London, 1950).
Heath, T. L., *A History of Greek Mathematics* (Oxford, 1931).
Heggie, D. C., *Megalithic Science* (London, 1981).
Herodotus, *The Histories* (Harmondsworth, 1972).
Hoffman, Banesh, and Dukes, Helen, *Albert Einstein* (New York, 1972).

Iamblichus, *A Life of Pythagoras,* tr. T. Taylor (London, 1818).
Kerenyi, C., *The Gods of the Greeks,* tr. Norman Cameron (London, 1951).
——, *Pythagoras and Orpheus* (Berlin, 1938).
Philip, J. A., *Pythagoras and the Early Pythagoreans* (University of Toronto, 1966).
Plato, *The Phaedo*
——, *The Republic*
——, *The Republic*
——, *The Meno*
Porphyry, *A Life of Pythagoras,* tr. T. Taylor (London 1818).
Raven, J. E., *Pythagoreans and Eleatics* (Amsterdam, 1966).
Richardson, Emeline Hill, *The Etruscans* (Chicago, 1976).
Scholem, Gershom, *Kabbalah* (Jerusalem, 1974).
Taylor, Thomas, *The Theoretic Arithmetic of the Pythagoreans* (1816, reprinted New York, 1972).
Yates, Frances, *The Rosicrucian Enlightenment* (London, 1972).
——, *Giordano Bruno and the Hermetic Tradition* (London, 1964).

INDEX